FINANCIAL SECTOR OF THE AMERICAN ECONOMY

edited by

STUART BRUCHEY
ALLAN NEVINS PROFESSOR EMERITUS
COLUMBIA UNIVERSITY

A GARLAND SERIES

STUDIES ON THE BEHAVIOR OF EQUITY MARKETS

ACHLA MARATHE

GARLAND PUBLISHING, Inc.
A MEMBER OF THE TAYLOR & FRANCIS GROUP
NEW YORK & LONDON / 1998

Library of Congress Cataloging-in-Publication Data

Marathe, Achla, 1966–
    Studies on the behavior of equity markets / Achla Marathe.
        p.   cm. — (Financial sector of the American economy)
    Includes bibliographical references and index.
    ISBN 0-8153-3329-3 (alk. paper)
    1. Stock exchanges. 2. Stock price forecasting. I. Title.
II. Series.
HG4551.M33 1998
332.63'222—dc21
                                                            98-46667

Printed on acid-free, 250-year-life paper
Manufactured in the United States of America

Contents

List of Tables

Preface

The efficiency, volatility and integration of the equity markets have always been a major concern to investors, financial analysts and academicians. This book provides a practical understanding of these issues with special applications to developed (primarily US) and developing countries. We look for new variables and models to predict and analyze US stock returns. Several comparisons are made between the US and emerging markets. The efficiency and integration tests done on emerging markets explore the potential for portfolio diversification. By exploiting the low correlations in returns between developed and developing countries and within developing countries, the reward to risk ratio of the portfolio can be significantly improved. We investigate whether the opening of emerging markets to foreign investors is facilitating the efficiency and integration of these markets with the global markets. In particular we perform a case study on the equity market in Korea to understand the extent of the impact of equity market liberalization on the domestic market fundamentals.

Several financial and economic variables have been tested to check the efficiency and predictability of the stock market. Aggregate output or GNP is frequently shown to have some explanatory power in predicting future stock returns. Chapter 2 of this book goes a step further in using aggregate output as a predictor of stock returns. It decomposes aggregate output into its permanent and temporary components which are associated with the real and monetary factors of the economy respectively. The empirical tests examine the explanatory power of each component and find that virtually all the predictability from aggregate output comes from the permanent component of output.

Chapter 3 looks at the risk-return relationship of the US stock market in recessionary and non recessionary time periods. Using a two regime switching regression model, it shows a highly significant negative relationship between excess returns and market volatility during recessionary market periods that tends to dominate the overall relationship. Chapter 4 discusses a trading strategy with which one might make modest trading profits under certain assumptions. It also provides clues as to how one might discriminate between small bubbles, large bubbles, small corrections and major market crashes.

Chapter 5 explores the relationship between the stock market and macroeconomic activity in the developing countries. Several tests are done to see if the equity markets are driven by the economic fundamentals of the respective country. We also examine whether the investors are being rewarded appropriately for bearing the systematic risk. Chapter 6 is a case study for Korea. The focus is on the liberalization of the equity market in Korea and its impact on the efficiency, volatility and integration of the domestic market.

There are several people whose extraordinary support and guidance was critical to this project. Dr. Hany Shawky did a great job in encouraging me and kept my momentum going. He coauthored Chapter 2 and Chapter 3 of this book which were published in *Quarterly Review of Economics and Finance* and *The Journal of Economics and Business* respectively. Dr. Bruce Dieffenbach was a great teacher. He taught me several courses in Monetary Economics and Finance which motivated me to do further research in this area. Dr. Edward Renshaw regularly helped me with his constructive suggestions and comments. An earlier version of Chapter 4 of this book appeared in *The Journal of Investing* which was coauthored with Dr. Renshaw.

I am grateful to Dr. Kwang Woo Jun of World Bank for sharing his ideas during my summer internship at *The World Bank*. He was instrumental in introducing me to the research in Emerging Markets. Chapter 5 and Chapter 6 are the products of the work I did under his supervision. Part of Chapter 6 appeared in the *World Bank Discussion Papers: Portfolio Investment in Developing Countries*.

I would like to extend a special thanks to my friends, Alferado Goyburu, Nipa Basu, Susmita Dasgupta, Sanjay Shah, Nlandu, Selcuk Caner, Shukla Mukherjee, Late Suneela Salgar, Rita Ganguly and Kaushik Chaudhary who often inspired me through their discussions and knowledge. I am deeply grateful to my family for their unwavering support and my husband Madhav, whose enthusiasm and encouragement led to the completion of this work.

Studies on the Behavior of Equity Markets

CHAPTER 1

Literature Survey

1.1 FINANCIAL MARKETS AND EFFICIENCY

The economic strength and the ability of a nation to gain the most from its accumulated human and natural resources requires well developed capital markets and institutions. There are many uses of the word *capital*. Economic capital represents assets primarily of a permanent nature, capital can also refer to the money value of the instruments of ownership and of long term claims to assets. Capital markets are the markets in which these instruments are exchanged. Capital markets comprise complex institutions and mechanisms through which intermediate-term funds and long-term funds are pooled and made available to business, governments and individuals. The capital market also encompasses the processes by which securities already outstanding are transferred.

Our aim is to analyze the behavior of capital markets. In capital markets, the area which has interested most economists and financial analysts is the price behavior of the securities market. In 1953, the *Royal Statistical Society* met in London to discuss a rather unusual paper i.e. "The Analysis of Economic Time Series." Its author Maurice Kendall was a distinguished statistician and the subject was behavior of stock and commodity prices. Kendall had been looking for regular price cycles but to his surprise he could not find them. Each series appeared to follow a random walk. The successive changes in price were independent or serially uncorrelated.

This discovery led to the concept of *market efficiency*. Market efficiency means all relevant and ascertainable information is reflected in security prices and no one can make economic profits based on readily available information. All investors have access to all the available information. If current price could be improved upon as a predictor of future prices using data on past returns or other macroeconomic variables such as money stock, output etc., it would suggest that capital markets are not informationally efficient. Investors could trade actively to exploit these correlations and hope to do better on average than investors who simply buy and hold. If however, markets are informationally efficient, then prices fully reflect available information and there are no exploitable correlations between future returns and current information. Mathematically, it can be expressed as:

$$P_t = \sum_{j=1}^{\infty} (1 + r)^{-j} E\left(d_{t+j}\right)$$

where P_t represents current asset price, r the market interest rate and d the dividend payments. This implies that the asset price should be equal to the discounted sum of the expected future payments. Most of the evidence accumulated on asset markets implied that they are informationally efficient. Fama's (1970) paper surveyed the empirical evidence available up to that date and established the conclusion in favor of market efficiency to most academic reader's satisfaction.

In efficient markets investors cannot possibly make economic profits. Economic profits mean profits in excess of the opportunity cost of capital. *Net present value* is the most known measure of the discounted value of the economic profits that any investment will produce. Since we notice plenty of projects with positive net present value, it would be appropriate to ask if positive net present value conflicts with the argument of market efficiency. The answer is "no." Any investment can have positive net present value if the company has some special advantage. Such advantages can arise in several ways. The company may be the first one to enter into the market with a new and improved product for which customers are prepared to pay premium prices. The premium will be paid until the competitors enter and squeeze out extra profits. The company may have a patent technology, production cost advantage, monopoly over some input or valuable contractual advantage that the competitors cannot match, at least for several years. All these factors can give rise to positive economic profits. Market efficiency only claims that security markets are efficient, it does not mean that other markets are efficient too and this could be the cause of positive economic profits.

1.1.1 Tests of Market Efficiency

Most of the early empirical research has been concentrated on whether prices "fully reflect" particular subsets of available information. The studies like Sidney (1961), Kleidon (1983), French and Roll (1986), Keim and Stambaugh (1986) Poterba and Summers (1987), Fama and French (1988) and Lo and McKinlay (1988) were concentrated on what we call *weak form* tests in which the information subset of interest is just past price histories. When extensive tests seemed to support the efficiency hypothesis at this level, attention was turned to *semi-strong form* tests in which the concern is the speed of adjustment to other publicly available information e.g. announcements of stock splits, annual reports, new security issues, dividends etc. Finally came *strong-form* tests in which the concern is whether any investor or group of investors have monopolistic access to certain information that enables them to make economic profits.

Major contributors to the area of market efficiency are Fama (1970), Pettit (1972), Fama and MacBeth (1973), Kon and Jen (1979), Patell and Wolfson (1984) and others who claim that markets are efficient. Fama and French (1988) in their classic paper concluded that markets are efficient only in the short run and not in the long run. Their empirical findings showed that returns over a period of 3 to 5 years were significantly correlated. Later a number of papers supported their results.

1.1.2 Do Economic Variables Explain Stock Price Behavior?

The studies that find returns to be predictable to some extent even in the short run do not deny that markets are efficient. Some such studies are by Fama (1970), Chen, Roll and Ross (1986), Keim and Stambaugh (1986), Campbell (1987), French, Schwert and Stambaugh (1987), Campbell and Shiller (1988), Lo and MacKinlay (1988) and more recently Fama (1990), Schwert (1990), Balvers, Cosimano and McDonald (1990) and Chen (1991). All of them have shown that variables like industrial production, risk premium defined as the spread between high grade and low grade bonds, term premium defined as the spread between the long term and the short term interest rates, dividend yield, inflation and price earnings ratio are empirically useful in predicting security returns.

Keim and Stambaugh (1986) find that expected risk premiums on many assets appear to change over time in a manner that is at least partially described by variables that reflect levels of asset prices. The variables considered in their study are risk premium, variation in S&P index and level of small stock prices. They also find returns on small firm stocks and low grade bonds are more highly correlated in January than in the rest of the year with previous levels of asset prices.

Chen, Roll and Ross (1986) test whether innovations in macroeconomic variables are risks that are rewarded in the stock market. They find economic variables like risk premium, term premium, expected and unexpected inflation and industrial production which systematically affect stock market returns are the sources of systematic risk that are significantly priced. They further claim that it is consistent with efficient market theory because asset prices should depend on their exposures to the state variables that describe the economy.

Fama and French (1989) find that expected returns of stocks and bonds contain default and term premium. They also show that default spread is high when business is persistently poor and low when the economy is persistently strong. The term premium is low near business cycle peaks and high near troughs. The above relationship implies that expected returns on financial assets are lower when economic conditions are strong and higher when economic conditions are weak.

Balvers, Cosimano and McDonald (1990) show empirically and theoretically that stock returns are a predictable function of aggregate output. They tested the following model assuming that output is a trend stationary series.

$$\ln R_{t+1} = \alpha + \beta_1 t + \beta_2 \ln y_t + u_t$$

Future stock returns were regressed on trend and the current level of output. They found the coefficient of lagged output to be significantly negative. More specifically, they show that expected returns are negatively related with current output. They justify their results by explaining that as consumption opportunities vary following variation in aggregate output, investors are faced with a less smooth consumption pattern. In attempting to smooth consumption, they adjust their investment and hence their required rate of return on financial assets. Because of this linkage, returns should be predictable to an extent related to the predictability of aggregate output. Fama (1990) finds that the growth rate of production, which is used as a proxy for shocks to expected cash flows, explains 43% of the annual return variance. Risk premium and term premium, which proxy for expected return shocks, capture 30% of the variance of annual value-weighted returns.

Chen (1991) studies the relationship between changes in financial investment opportunities and changes in the macroeconomy. He shows that state variables like the lagged production growth rate, the default premium, the term premium, the short-term interest rate and the market dividend price ratio are indicators of recent and future economic growth. He further shows that market excess returns are negatively correlated with recent economic growth and positively correlated with expected future economic growth.

All these studies have found that stock returns are predictable to some extent even in the short run, yet they still support the notion of market efficiency. Variation in asset prices depend on their exposure to economic variables which describe the economy. The variation in these variables being the source of systematic risk causes the variation in stock prices.

1.2 STOCK MARKET VOLATILITY

The U.S. financial markets have experienced substantial volatility. The U.S. public became very sensitive to the negative aspects of market volatility after the stock market crash in October 1987 and the bout of market turbulence in October 1989. These events have led financial economists to write numerous scientific papers on market volatility and the stock market mechanism. A few of them are Kenneth (1988), Kindleberger (1989), Schwert (1989), Ferson and Harvey (1991), LeRoy and Parke (1992) and Roll (1992). Some other classic papers on volatility were written by Shiller (1979, 1981a, 1981b), Grossman and Shiller (1981), Poterba and Summers (1986), Marsh and Merton (1986). In addition, various regulatory agencies and exchanges have commissioned reports to investigate the crash of 1987.

Although these studies have provided new insights into the working of the stock market, there is still considerable controversy about the causes and consequences of market volatility and the merits of proposed regulations. Even the definition of volatility varies greatly.

One simple way of defining *volatility* is that it is an indicator of the riskiness of the asset it represents. For example common stocks are more volatile and hence much riskier capital assets than treasury bills.

Wendy Gramm pointed out that some people hold that only a large downward price movement constitutes volatility, while an upward price movement is simply a *recovery*. What this distinction ignores is that liquid markets need people on both sides of the market, buyers and sellers. While price volatility can be measured in a number of ways such as the price range or variance of price changes, it is important to consider both the upward and downward movements in the price index. James Tobin points out that the only volatility that should matter to portfolio managers is the covariance of stock returns with their entire portfolio of assets. Hence it is the *co-volatility* which is the important economic concern and not just volatility.

1.2.1 Why do we care about volatility?

The importance of volatility is best described in Tobin (1992). He says, a one day drop of 20% in stock prices makes us wonder whether the market is doing a good job in performing its social role as an allocator of resources. It seems to question the usefulness of the *signals* the market is sending to savers and businesses about where to invest their capital.

If the market gives wrong signals at different times, its volatility could be exaggerating the risk of corporate investment. That is, if there is significantly more volatility in corporate stock prices than in the fundamental corporate earnings stream, stock price volatility could increase risks to market investors out of all proportion to the economic risks of corporate investment. This could raise the cost of capital to the firm and cause the equity prices to be lower than they should be and hence reduce corporate real investment.

For fundamentally oriented money managers, volatility can make it very hard to execute orders. Corporate executives will not be happy if the stock price does not reflect the company's fundamentals. High volatility can put stock brokers in trouble. They have no way to explain the episodes of excessive volatility to their clients. Ultimately, volatility could undermine the confidence of general public. If investors see that their wealth can drop by 23% in one day in October 1987, their future investment behavior is likely to be influenced by their past memories.

1.2.2 Is volatility consistent with market efficiency?

Some economists have argued that volatility is not necessarily a market problem. It is true that prices are now more responsive to market developments but such price movements are the consequences of markets that are better able to reflect ongoing changes in fundamental factors that affect supply and demand. As more sources of information become available and the methods for processing information improve, trading will almost certainly rise. If prices change in response to more frequent revision of investors' valuations, then more trading is likely to result in greater reported intra-day volatility. To the extent, increased volatility is simply a reflection of the more frequent arrival and processing of new information, it is fully consistent with market efficiency. No volatility means that prices are unable to adjust to changes in information regarding supply and demand.

In the words of Richard Roll, when investors see large price changes, they become more or less fearful; and they suddenly increase and decrease their required rate of returns on risky assets, thus leading to immediate and sometimes fairly significant changes in prices. If we could tell when investors were going to raise or lower their discount rates above or below some long-run norm, we could exploit their behavior to make money. In that case it would be justified to say that markets were not efficient. But if there is nothing investors can exploit in a systematic way, it is hard to say that markets are inefficient. A true market inefficiency ought to provide an exploitable opportunity. Richard Roll though agrees that there are psychological factors apart from fundamentals that affect the stock prices, he shows that there is no consistent way of taking advantage of these factors and beating the market.

Robert Shiller (1981) however shows that the volatility of stock prices could not be explained by the volatility of *fundamentals* such as corporate dividends and earnings and hence markets cannot possibly be as efficient as the financial economists suggest. It is similar to the Grossman and Stiglitz *paradox* which suggested that markets cannot be efficient because if current prices truly incorporated all available information, and everyone believed this to be so, then no one would have an incentive to produce information. How could markets then be kept efficient? Shiller posed a similar question. He said if stock prices reflect the discounted value of all expected future dividends, then why are stock prices so much more volatile than dividends. Surely the possibility of changes in the interest rate and the growth rates, the only missing variables in his equation, could not account for the volatility observed in the stock prices. So he does not believe in the economic and fundamental-based explanation of stock price movement.

Merton Miller's response to Shiller is that with securities of long duration like common stocks, even modest changes in expected dividend growth and discount rate could lead to significant changes in value. He used Gordon's dividend discount model, which says that stock price (V) equals the current dividend (D) divided by the discount rate (r) minus the dividend growth rate (g). In equation form:

$$V = \frac{D}{r - g}$$

In his numerical example, Miller showed that just by raising 'r' and lowering 'g' by half a percent each, the investors' estimate of the value of the firm could be reduced by 25%.

However, Shiller's belief is that during the 1987 crash there was no change in either 'r' or 'g' and the only reason the crash occured was a *speculative bubble*, which is of course inconsistent with the notion of market efficiency. According to him, people were selling simply because they thought other people were going to sell. So psychological behavior is the most important cause of the crash.

1.2.3 Shiller's Variance Bounds Test

As argued earlier, Robert Shiller (1981) provided significant evidence that stock market volatility in general, cannot be explained by movements in the rational expectation of future dividends and interest rates. He claims economic and fundamental based explanation of price movement has not been able to explain excess volatility. He supports Fischer Black's statement that stock prices lie most of the time between half and twice their fundamental values.

Shiller's simplest *variance-bounds* inequality says that the price of stock should be less volatile than the present value of actual future dividends, assuming that the former can be taken to equal the conditional expectations of the latter. This is so because the price of stock equals the present value of dividends less a forecast error which under rational expectations is orthogonal to price. Therefore, the variance of the ex-post rational stock price should exceed the variance of the actual price by an amount equal to the variance of the forecast error. In other words,

$$P_t = E(\hat{P}_t)$$

$$\hat{P}_t = P_t + u_t$$

$$var(\hat{P}_t) = var(P_t) + var(u_t)$$

P_t is the actual price, $\hat{P}_t$ is the forecasted price, u_t is the forecast error, the covariance between P_t and u_t is zero. So,

$$var(\hat{P}_t) \geq var(P_t)$$

One econometric problem Shiller encountered was that the price series was not stationary. In order to attain stationarity Shiller (1981) fitted a log linear trend to stock prices and took the residuals from this trend to be the series restricted by the variance bounds inequalities. He then tested the above inequality and found exactly the opposite result. The inequality was violated by the data.

Shiller's findings sparked substantial controversy. Marsh and Merton (1986) disputed his claim while Mankiw, Romer and Shapiro (1985) provided supporting evidence. LeRoy and Porter (1981) suggested a different correction to attain stationarity. They assumed that the trend in prices was attributable to inflation and retained earnings and implemented a procedure to reverse the effects of these factors on stock prices. Subsequent criticism indicated that both procedures were flawed. Allan Kleidon (1986) showed that if the underlying price series has a unit root, then the supposedly trend adjusted series as calculated by Shiller (1979, 1981) will still be non-stationary. Further, if the variance bounds tests are implemented despite the non-stationarity of the underlying series, they will be strongly biased towards rejection. Marsh and Merton (1986) also objected to the assumption of trend-stationary price series.

An alternative explanation to Shiller's theory was suggested by Burton Malkiel (1979) and Pindyck (1984) in connection with the significant decline in real stock market values between the mid 1960's and the early 1980's. They argued that market movements reflect, in substantial part, changing risk premia induced by movements in stock market volatility. So changes in risk are responsible for a significant part of the variation in security prices.

Poterba and Summers (1986) examined the changing risk hypothesis and the influence of changing stock market volatility on the level of stock prices. They found that shocks to volatility decayed rapidly and therefore could affect required returns for only short intervals. This implies volatility shocks can have only a small impact on stock market prices and therefore we cannot claim that volatility induced fluctuations in risk premia account for much of the observed variation in stock prices.

1.3 RELATIONSHIP BETWEEN RISK AND RETURN

There have been many studies which examined the relationship between stock returns and market volatility. The research started as early as in 1952 when Harry Markowitz (1952), following Von Neumann and Morgenstern developed an analysis based on the expected utility maxim and proposed a general solution for the portfolio problem. Assuming that investors consider expected return a desirable thing and variance of return as an undesirable thing, we can use this as a rule in the selection of securities. Once the mean and variance of each security is calculated, the set of efficient *mean-variance* combination could be computed. The investor could select the combination he preferred and the portfolio which gave rise to this mean-variance combination can be found.

Tobin (1958) showed that under certain conditions Markowitz's model implies that the process of investment choice can be broken down into two phases. First, the choice of a unique optimum combination of risky assets and second, a separate choice concerning the allocation of funds between such a combination and a single riskless asset.

Markowitz and Tobin concentrated their work mostly on the investor behavior while Sharpe (1964) constructed a market equilibrium theory of asset prices under conditions of risk. This theory's implications were consistent with the assertions of the traditional financial theory of Markowitz. Sharpe in his *capital asset pricing model* showed that a higher expected rate of return on holdings can be attained only by incurring additional risk. In fact, the market pays two kinds of prices; the *price of time* or the pure interest rate and the *price of risk*, the additional expected return per unit of risk borne. The risk-return relationship can be described by the following equation:

$$R_i = R_f + (R_m - R_f)\beta_i + u_i$$

where R_i is the return on security i, R_f is the risk free rate, R_m is the return on the market portfolio, $\beta_i = \text{Cov}(R_i, R_m)/\text{Var}(R_m)$ is the systematic risk and u_i is the unsystematic risk. The basic implications of CAPM model are:

1. Investment in any asset contains two types of risk; *systematic risk and unsystematic risk*. Systematic risk is the risk related to the market which cannot be diversified away. Unsystematic risk is the company or firm specific risk which can be diversified away.

2. $E(R_i) > 0$

3. $E(R_m) > 0$

According to CAPM every investor buys an efficient market portfolio which consists of all the assets unlike the traditional approach in which degree of risk aversion determines the type of asset bought. Risk averse people buy less risky assets while risk lovers buy more risky assets.

Fama and MacBeth (1973) show that there is a positive tradeoff between return and risk, with risk measured from the portfolio viewpoint. Also, while making a portfolio decision, an investor should assume that the relationship between the expected return on a security and its risk in any efficient portfolio is linear. They also supported Sharpe's theory that there is no risk, in addition to portfolio risk which systematically affects average returns.

French, Schwert and Stambaugh (1987) studied the relationship between expected risk premium and different components of volatility. Volatility, which is measured by the standard deviation in stock returns, is separated into two components, predictable and unpredictable volatility using *autoregressive integrated moving average* (ARIMA) models.

Regressions of monthly excess holding period return on the predictable component provided little evidence of a positive relation between *ex-ante* volatility and expected risk premium. However, they found a strong negative relation between excess holding period return and the unpredictable component of volatility. They interpreted this negative relation as an indirect evidence of a positive relation between the predictable component of volatility and the excess holding period return. The reason being that if the risk premium is positively related to the predicted standard deviation, the discount rate for future cash flow will increase. If the cash flows are unaffected, the higher discount rate will reduce both the current present value and the stock price. This implies that a positive *ex-ante* relation induces a negative relation between expected return and the unpredictable component of volatility.

Robert Merton (1980) pointed out that there has been little research on estimating expected return. The current practice for estimating the expected market return is to add the historical average realized excess market returns to the current observed interest rate. While this model explicitly reflects the dependence of the market return on the interest rate, it fails to account for the effect of changes in the level of market risk. Merton suggests that while estimating models of the expected return, the non-negativity restriction of the expected excess return should be explicitly included as part of the specification. Secondly, estimators which use realized returns should be adjusted for heteroskedasticity, though he agrees that estimators based on the assumption of constant variance will also give consistent results.

1.4 EMERGING STOCK MARKETS

"Emerging markets" are defined as the markets in the developing economies which have the potential for development. Argentina, Brazil, Chile, Colombia, Greece, India, Indonesia, Pakistan, Portugal, Philippines, Turkey, Malaysia, Mexico, Thailand, Venezuela and Zimbabwe are a few of them. Emerging markets are large and expanding rapidly but they continue to exhibit very different risk and return characteristics than comparably-sized developed markets. The combination of high yields, highly autocorrelated returns and volatile prices suggest that these markets may be inefficient, have excess returns and may not be fully integrated into global capital markets. More importantly, as pointed out by Buckberg (1992), consistently high rates of return in these countries translate into a high cost of capital, which limits the stock markets' role as a source of private financing.

To a considerable extent this may be explained by the existence of substantial barriers to access. In many cases foreign portfolio investment is permitted only through country funds, closed-end trust funds etc. There is a general limit on equity and bond investment by foreigners and also significant tax disincentives.

However, a growing number of developing countries are becoming aware of the potential benefits of attracting foreign savings in the form of portfolio investment. This could result in significant restructuring of international portfolios, first, because emerging stock markets would become more accessible and second, the removal of restrictions would change asset prices in these markets. While currently, stock prices in some emerging markets tend to move in opposite directions from the S&P composite index or the Japan's Nikkei index thus enabling investors to achieve higher returns for a given level of risk, the integration of these markets would imply that price movements would become more closely linked to movements in other markets. Cornelius (1992) found that capital controls are very effective at insulating the domestic market from foreign disturbances. However, in the case of Korea, market segmentation was not complete due to the strong economic ties with other countries.

Buckberg (1992) investigates whether emerging markets are now part of the world financial markets and why they behave differently than developed markets. Out of the twenty emerging markets analyzed in the study, fourteen were consistent with the *International Capital Asset Pricing* model for the years 1985 to 1991. Tests on the earlier data indicated that few emerging markets were integrated prior to 1984. Highly autocorrelated returns suggest that lagged prices may contain exploitable information about future returns. She also found evidence of predictability-widely interpreted as evidence of speculative inefficiency in developed markets.

Errunza and Losq (1985) examined the behavior of stock prices of Argentina, Brazil, Chile, Greece, India, Korea, Jordan, Mexico, Thailand and Zimbabwe. They concluded, based on probability distributions, run tests and serial correlation coefficients that, by and large, emerging markets even though not as efficient as major developed markets, are quite comparable to the smaller European markets like Netherlands, Belgium and Sweden.

Santis (1993) measured the benefits of diversification for emerging markets by testing the traditional mean-variance frontier for asset returns. The correlation structure of the emerging markets and the estimated volatility bounds reveal that considerable gains from diversification are still available to investors. Portfolios which include assets from emerging markets outperformed portfolios which included only U.S. assets or U.S. assets combined with other indexes for developed countries.

1.5 INTERNATIONALIZATION OF THE KOREAN EQUITY MARKET

1.5.1 Foreign Investment Policy

Until the late 1950's foreign investment in Korean equity markets was not allowed. The main factors were apprehension related to the Japanese colonial period and a bad investment climate. In January 1960, the legal base of foreign investment was provided through the enactment of the *Foreign Capital Inducement Promotion Act*. The basic principle was to allow any form of bona fide foreign capital to enter Korea. This liberal policy lasted until 1965 when the Republic of Korea normalized diplomatic relations with Japan. In 1965 the government introduced various measures to regulate the quality of foreign capital but they were not implemented till 1973. The most important measure, joint ventures, where the firms are partially owned by the domestic investors and partially by the foreign investors, began to receive greater priority than the firms which were completely owned by the foreigners. A very specific guideline for foreign direct investment was adopted. The eligibility criteria designated the following projects as ineligible for approval:

1. Projects that would disrupt domestic demand and supply of raw materials and intermediate products.

2. Projects that would compete in overseas markets with domestic firms.

3. Projects that would aim only at profiting from land use.

The foreign participation ratio was limited to 50% except in a few cases. Also, domestic participation of more than 50% was required if the projects were very labor intensive, dependent on domestic sources for major raw materials and oriented towards local market sales.

   The government of Korea has gradually liberalized its foreign investment policy since 1980. The *Foreign Capital Inducement Act* was revised in December 1984 to encourage foreign direct investment in equity markets. There were two main reasons for the changes in the foreign investment law. *First*, the government felt that the regulations governing foreign direct investment and technology inducement contracts needed to be reduced in order to promote those activities. The government of Korea had relied heavily on loans as a source of foreign capital and on technology licensing as a source of foreign technology. As a result of this policy of promoting unpackaging of capital and technology, the ratio of foreign direct investment in capital markets in Korea to the size of the economy was much smaller than for other *New Industrial Countries*. *Secondly*, the percentage of equity forms of investment to the total outstanding debt was also very small by international standards. In 1983, the foreign direct investment in equity markets was just 2.7% of the total foreign debt. The *third* major reason for the change was government's realization that tax exemption offered to foreign investment may result in a loss of tax revenue without much incentive effects, given the taxation by the source country of foreign earned income.

From 1986 to 1988, the Korean securities market expanded both in quality and quantity. The composite stock price index (CSPI) increased from 67% in 1986, 93% in 1987 and 70% in 1988. The continuous rise in the index reflected steady growth of the Korean economy. The affluence in the economy pushed down Korea's interest rates, hence helping the securities market grow further. In 1989 the difference between the domestic and foreign interest rate was still very high. Also, the won appreciated against the U.S. dollar by more than 30%. This made the market look very attractive to foreigners for investment purposes. Because of the high returns in the Korean market, the government had to take measures to protect it from foreign investors.

If the market had been opened at that time, a sudden inflow of money to take advantage of the high yields would have deprived Koreans of the chance to benefit from the growing stock market. In 1989 the government laid out a plan which suggested gradual opening of the market to foreign direct investment by the year 1992 but limited to a certain extent. Also, Korean institutional investors such as banks, securities and insurance firms would have higher limits to invest in overseas securities.

The stock market performance was very bearish in 1989. On December 12, CSPI hit 844.75 which was the lowest for the year to that point. The Ministry of Finance panicked and announced a series of measures designed to stabilize the capital market. Highlights included:

1. Balancing supply and demand mostly by forcing institutions to purchase stocks.

2. Prearranging the number and timing of companies going public.

3. Asking banks and central banks to loan an unrestricted amount of funds to investors if necessary.

4. The government raised the interest rate on deposits at securities companies, from 1% to 5% to attract potential investors in stocks and securities companies rather than commercial banks, which paid higher interest on savings.

5. The government also emphasized its intentions to follow through the liberalization plan by 1992.

Until 1989 the government restricted Korean companies from borrowing outside the country, fearing that the resulting increase in the money supply would cause inflation to rise. But high interest rates made it expensive to borrow domestically. The government relented allowing many corporations to raise debt more cheaply in the international capital market. In 1990 and 1991 the stock market remained bearish. Until 1991 foreign securities firms were only allowed to hold a maximum 10% equity portion in a joint venture. The companies which already had joint venture firms were allowed to increase their share in these ventures to 40% on an aggregate basis.

1.5.2 The Final Step Towards Liberalization

The 1992 plan for the opening of the Korean stock market to foreign investment represents the final step in the government's internationalization of the domestic securities market making Korea the biggest emerging market. This permits direct purchases by foreigners of the shares listed on the Korea stock exchange subject to the following conditions:

1. No single foreign investor can have more than 3% of the total outstanding shares of any listed company.

2. Aggregate foreign ownership is limited to 10% of the total outstanding shares of each class and each listed company. In certain cases the limit is only 8%. The lower limit is applied to companies considered important for public interest.

The official statistics show that by the end of March 1993, 1800 foreign investors from 38 countries had brought new investment funds totaling $4.2 billion equivalent. Investors from the U.K. represented the largest portion (38.5%) of equity investment inflows, followed by U.S. (30.7%) and New Zealand (5.5%). Through March 1993, the total number of Korean equity shares held by foreign investors was 156 million with a market value close to W3 trillion.

NOTE

1. See Tobin et al. (1992).

CHAPTER 2

Predicting Stock Returns Using Different Components of Output

2.1 INTRODUCTION

There is a growing body of literature on the predictability of stock and bond returns using macroeconomic variables.[1] Studies that document such predictability are, for example, Fama and French (1988), Keim and Stambaugh (1986), Campbell (1987), French, Schwert and Stambaugh (1987), Campbell and Shiller (1988), Chen, Roll and Ross (1986), Lo and MacKinlay (1988), Fama and French (1989), and more recently Fama (1990), Schwert (1990), Balvers, Cosimano and McDonald (1990) and Chen (1991). These studies have shown that state variables such as aggregate production growth, yield spreads between long and short term government bonds, yield spreads between low grade and high grade bonds, unexpected inflation and dividend yields are empirically useful in forecasting stock and bond returns.

The predictability of stock returns using industrial production or aggregate output is the primary focus of this chapter. Instead of using aggregate output as the state variable we first decompose aggregate output into its permanent and transitory components. The purpose is to examine the significance of each component in forecasting stock returns. Aggregate output is a non-stationary series characterized as a difference stationary process which can be decomposed into a stochastic trend and a stationary component. The trend component is modeled as a random walk with parameters estimated using an autoregressive integrated moving average (ARIMA) representation.[2]

The permanent or growth component is the stochastic trend in the series which contributes substantially to the long run variation in output and is characterized within the framework of growth theory. The shocks to the permanent component are assumed to be associated with changes in the real factors in the economy like capital accumulation, population growth and technological change. The transitory component is the stationary part of the series and is assumed to be affected more by the monetary factors in the economy.[3]

While Fama and French (1988), Balvers, Cosimano and McDonald (1990), Chen (1991) and others have argued that in the context of intertemporal models, predictability of stock returns using aggregate output is not necessarily inconsistent with the notion of market efficiency, a more compelling argument can be made regarding the predictability of stock returns using different components of output. Specifically, if the permanent component of output which is associated with the real factors in the economy proves useful in forecasting stock returns, that would be consistent with market efficiency. On the other hand, the transitory component of output which is associated with monetary and fiscal disturbances in the economy is not expected to be related to real stock returns.

This chapter proceeds as follows. Section II describes the data and various proxies. Section III reproduces some of the existing evidence regarding the relationship between expected returns and aggregate output. Section IV shows the decomposition of aggregate output into its permanent and transitory components and provides some empirical results for the predictive ability of both the components of output. The final section provides a brief summary and some concluding remarks.

2.2 DATA

Common stock returns are represented by the return series on the *S&P* 500 composite index, the CRSP value-weighted and equal-weighted portfolios. Daily CRSP portfolio returns were obtained from the Center for Research in Security Prices (CRSP) for the years 1962 through 1990 whereas the monthly *S&P* 500 composite returns were obtained from the CITIBASE data for the years 1947 to 1990. The daily returns of both value and equal weighted portfolios are converted into continuously compounded monthly, quarterly and yearly returns. To convert the nominal returns into real, the inflation rate measured by the change in Consumer Price Index is used. Monthly data for the CPI and seasonally adjusted industrial production was obtained from CITIBASE data. Industrial production was used to represent the output variable. The figures for the quarterly and yearly data for industrial production were derived from the monthly observations reported in the CITIBASE data.

2.3   RELATION BETWEEN EXPECTED RETURNS AND AGGREGATE OUTPUT

Expected returns on financial assets contain risk and time premia. Risk or default premium compensates for the sensitivity of returns to unexpected changes in business conditions whereas time or maturity premium compensates for exposure to discount rate shocks. Both premia are inversely related to general economic conditions. When business conditions are persistently poor, expected premia are high because agents require a higher premium to induce them to invest in risky assets. When business conditions are persistently strong expected premia are low because agents can be induced to invest at much lower premia (see Chen, Roll and Ross (1986), Fama and French (1989) and Chen (1991)). Since expected term and default premia are inversely related to the current economic conditions, a positive correlation between market returns and term and default premia implies that future market returns are also inversely related to current economic conditions. Hence, if aggregate output is used as a proxy for economic condition, we should apriori expect to observe a negative relation between market returns and lagged output.

There is another plausible explanation for the negative relation between expected returns and economic conditions. Fama and French (1989) and Balvers, Cosimano and McDonald (1990) argue that when the business cycle is at its peak and aggregate output is high, people have high income relative to their wealth. According to the Life Cycle Permanent Income hypothesis of Modigliani and Brumberg (1955), people tend to smooth their consumption patterns by saving into future periods when income might be low. This implies that in periods of high income, agents should have a high propensity to save and hence high investment. Similarly, when output is low and income is low, agents should have a low propensity to save and therefore low investment. Hence the argument goes that during good (poor) economic conditions when investment is high (low), the future capital stock is high (low) and the marginal productivity of capital is low (high), the returns on financial assets should be low (high).

To examine this relationship, we employ two alternative measures of output. First, we use the log of output series as the state variable as was adopted by Balvers, Cosimano and McDonald (1990) and theoretically justified based on their general equilibrium model.[4] This approach implicitly assumes that the aggregate output series follows a trend stationary process, the regression model estimated is then:

$$\ln R_{t+1} = C + \alpha_1 \text{trend} + \alpha_2 \ln y_t + \xi_{t+1} \tag{2.1}$$

where R_{t+1} is one plus the continuously compounded return on CRSP market portfolio in period $t + 1$ minus the inflation measured by the change in CPI, y_t is the seasonally adjusted industrial output in real terms in period t.[5] Table 2.1 presents the parameter estimates of equation (2.1) for three different horizons. Panels A, B and C give the estimates for the value-weighted, equal-weighted and $S\&P$ 500 composite returns.

For the value-weighted, equal-weighted as well as the $S\&P$ portfolio returns, the coefficient of the lagged output variable is negative and statistically significant for all time horizons. Though $S\&P$ 500 composite index returns exhibit the most significant relation with the lagged output, equal-weighted portfolio returns are most sensitive to the lagged output. The R^2 increases as the time measurement interval increases. These results are consistent with those found by Balvers, Cosimano and McDonald (1990).

Alternatively, we use the rate of growth of output as employed by Fama and French (1989), Fama (1990) and Chen (1991) to represent the state variable. This approach implicitly assumes that the output series follows a difference stationary process. Indeed, the rate of growth of output is a stationary series that exhibits convergence.[6]

As in Chen (1991), the economic condition is being measured by the growth rate of output over the previous 12 months.[7] That is, the growth rate of output for period t is calculated as

$$Gy_t = \log[y_t / y_{t-12}]$$

Table 2.1: Regression Estimates of the Relation Between Future Stock Returns and Aggregate Output

$$\ln R_{t+1} = C + \alpha_1 \text{trend} + \alpha_2 \ln y_t + \xi_{t+1}$$

	C	α_1	α_2	N	R^2
Panel A: VW CRSP					
Monthly	0.58	.0003	-0.14	342	0.26
	(3.08)	(2.98)	(3.05)		
Quarterly	1.70	.003	-.041	114	.07
	(2.92)	(2.83)	(2.90)		
Yearly	5.37	0.04	-1.31	28	.20
	(2.52)	(2.47)	(2.50)		
Panel B: EW CRSP					
Monthly	0.69	.0004	-0.16	342	.02
	(2.77)	(2.50)	(2.72)		
Quarterly	2.04	.003	-0.48	114	.05
	(2.42)	(2.19)	(2.37)		
Yearly	6.30	0.04	-1.51	28	.13
	(1.91)	(1.70)	(1.86)		
Panel C: *S&P* 500					
Monthly	0.29	.0002	-0.08	527	.03
	(4.26)	(3.92)	(4.16)		
Quarterly	0.88	.002	-0.25	175	.07
	(3.52)	(3.23)	(3.44)		
Yearly	3.39	0.03	-0.98	43	.24
	(3.51)	(3.21)	(3.42)		

Table 2.2: Regression Estimates of the Relation Between Future Stock Returns and the Growth Rate in Aggregate Output

$$\ln R_{t+1} = C' + \gamma_1 Gy_t + u_{t+1}$$

	C'	γ_1	N	R^2
Panel A: VW CRSP				
Monthly	0.006	-0.21	342	.007
	(2.15)	(1.60)		
Quarterly	0.02	-0.94	114	.04
	(2.32)	(2.16)		
Yearly	0.06	-2.06	28	.07
	(1.96)	(1.47)		
Panel B: EW CRSP				
Monthly	0.01	-.036	342	.01
	(3.40)	(2.07)		
Quarterly	0.04	-1.60	114	.05
	(3.34)	(2.60)		
Yearly	0.14	-3.42	28	.09
	(2.94)	(1.67)		
Panel C: *S&P* 500				
Monthly	0.006	-.07	515	.01
	(3.72)	(2.92)		
Quarterly	0.02	-0.23	171	.04
	(3.01)	(2.61)		
Yearly	0.07	-0.92	42	.13
	(2.80)	(2.42)		

where y_t is the level of aggregate output for month t. Using the growth rate of aggregate output as the state variable, we run the following regression:

$$\ln R_{t+1} = C' + \gamma_1 G y_t + u_{t+1} \qquad (2.2)$$

where R_{t+1} is the real market return in period t+1 and Gy_t is the growth rate of aggregate output in period t.[8] Table 2.2 presents the parameter estimates of equation (2.2). Panel A, B and C provide estimates using the value-weighted, equal-weighted and *S&P* 500 composite returns respectively.

For all, the value-weighted, equal-weighted and *S&P* 500 portfolio returns, the coefficients of the lagged output variable are again negative and statistically significant for almost all time horizons. The equal-weighted portfolio still responds most to the lagged output however *S&P* 500 composite index returns show the highest level of significance. The R^2 again increases as the time measurement interval increases. These results are similar to those obtained by Chen (1991).

The similarity of the results in Table 2.1 and Table 2.2 above indicates that regardless of how one measures the aggregate output, there is a persistent inverse relationship between expected returns on financial assets and output.[9] If real output is an indicator of economic conditions we can conclude that expected stock returns are inversely related to economic conditions.

2.4 DECOMPOSITION OF OUTPUT INTO PERMANENT AND TRANSITORY COMPONENTS

2.4.1 Background on Decomposition

A number of approaches to numerical decomposition of macroeconomic series have been suggested in literature. One method assumes trend is a deterministic linear or polynomial function of time. The stationary or cyclical component emerges in this method as a residual from the trend line. A rather unsatisfactory implication of this approach is that long run evolution of the time series is deterministic and therefore perfectly predictable. For instance:

$$x_t = a_1 t + a_2 t^2 + z_t$$

x_t becomes fully predictable if we just insert the right value of t to determine the trend part. We already know that the best forecast of the stationary part z_t is zero. Imposing a deterministic trend on a series which actually follows a random process and deviates from the deterministic trend without bound, can severely distort the statistical properties of the macroeconomic series.

A large number of studies including Beveridge and Nelson (1981) have shown that many economic time series are well represented by the class of homogeneous non stationary ARIMA processes for which the first differences are a stationary process of autoregressive moving average form. This approach implies that the accurate long run forecast of the series can not be made. The forecast error rises as we forecast further into the future. The best forecast is the current value. For example if:

$$x_t = x_t^p + x_t^t$$
$$x_t^p = x_{t-1}^p + e_t$$
$$x_t^p = \lim_{n \to \infty} E_t\left(x_{t+n}^p\right)$$

where x_t^p is the random walk component and x_t^t is the stationary component.

$$var(x_t) = var\left(x_t^p\right) + var\left(x_t^t\right)$$
$$var(x_t) = tvar(e_t) + var\left(x_t^t\right)$$

Clearly the variance of the permanent component is a function of time but the variance of the stationary component is not. Campbell and Mankiw (1987) criticized the random walk component model and claimed that one cannot make inferences about long run behavior of a economic series by looking primarily at the short run. According to Cochrane (1988) the random walk component is a property of all autocorrelations taken together but conventional procedures concentrate on the first few autocorrelations in order to capture the short run dynamics. We know:

$$\frac{1}{k} \lim_{k \to \infty} var(x_t - x_{t-k}) = var(\Delta x_t^p)$$

because

$$var(x_t - x_{t-k}) = k\sigma^2$$

but if $(x_t - x_{t-1})$ and $(x_{t-1} - x_{t-2})$ are positively correlated then

$$\frac{var(x_t - x_{t-2})}{2} > var(x_t - x_{t-1})$$

Cochrane (1988) believed that a plausible model for an economic series like GNP may have a combination of both components; i.e. a small random walk component and trend component.

2.4.2 Decomposition of Output into Permanent and Transitory Components

Any time series which exhibits the kind of homogeneous non-stationarity typical of economic time series can be decomposed into two additive components; a time trend and a stationary process or, a random walk and a stationary process. The first is known as a trend stationary process and the second is a difference stationary process.[10] The aggregate output series, characterized as a difference stationary process can be decomposed based on the following model.[11] Let the first difference of log of output Δy_t follow a vector autoregression such that:

$$\Delta y_t = a + A_1 \Delta y_{t-1} + \cdots + A_n \Delta y_{t-n} + e_t \qquad (2.3)$$

which can be written as

$$A(L)\Delta y_t = a + e_t \qquad (2.4)$$

where

$$A(L) = 1 - A_1 L - A_2 L^2 - \cdots - A_n L^n$$

also,

$$\Delta y_t = A(L)^{-1}[a + e_t] \qquad (2.5)$$

Equation (2.5) can be broken into two parts, the random walk component y_t^p and the stationary component y_t^t. The random walk component contains the unitary root and the stationary part contains all the roots greater than one in absolute value. The equation for Δy_t^p, which is also derived in Beveridge and Nelson (1981) can be written as

$$\Delta y_t^p = A(1)^{-1}[a + e_t] \qquad (2.6)$$

The equation for the transitory or the stationary component is obtained when $|L| > 1$ i.e.

$$\Delta y_t^t = A^*(L)^{-1}[a + e_t] \qquad (2.7)$$

where $A^*(L)$ contains all the roots greater than one in absolute value.
Equation (2.4) can be written as

$$A(L)(1-L)y_t = a + e_t$$
$$A(L)(1-L)\left(y_t^t + y_t^p\right) = a + e_t$$
$$A(L)(1-L)y_t^t = a + e_t - A(L)(1-L)y_t^p$$
$$= a + e_t - A(L)\Delta y_t^p \qquad (2.8)$$
$$= a + e_t - A(L)[A(1)]^{-1}[a + e_t] \quad \text{(using(2.6))}$$
$$= a - A(L)[A(1)]^{-1}a + e_t - A(L)[A(1)]^{-1}e_t \quad (2.9)$$

and since,

$$a - A(L)[A(1)]^{-1}a = 0$$

we obtain,

$$A(L)(1-L)y_t^t = \left[1 - A(L)[A(1)]^{-1}\right]e_t \qquad (2.10)$$

The R.H.S. of equation (2.9) can be factored as

$$1 - A(L)[A(1)]^{-1} = (1 - L)B(L) \qquad (2.11)$$

using L' Hopital's rule we have

$$B(1) = \lim_{L \to \infty} \frac{1 - [A(1)]^{-1}A(L)}{1 - L} = A'(1)[A(1)]^{-1} \qquad (2.12)$$

since by definition

$$y_t^p = y_t - y_t^t$$

$$
\begin{aligned}
y_t^p &= y_t - [A(L)]^{-1}B(L)e_t \quad \big(\text{using (2.9) and (2.10)}\big) \\
&= y_t - [A(L)]^{-1}B(L)[(1 - L)A(L)y_t - a] \quad \big(\text{using (2.8)}\big) \\
&= [1 - (1 - L)B(L)]y_t + [A(L)]^{-1}B(L)a \\
&= [A(1)]^{-1}A(L)y_t + [A(1)]^{-1}B(1)a \quad \big(\text{using (2.10) and (2.11)}\big)(2.13)
\end{aligned}
$$

Hence,

$$y_t^p = [A(1)]^{-1}A(L)y_t + [A(1)]^{-1}A'(1)[A(1)]^{-1}a \qquad (2.14)$$

Equation (2.14) is the expression for the permanent component of output. Since aggregate output is the sum of the transitory and the permanent component, the transitory component can be calculated as

$$y_t^t = y_t - y_t^p \qquad (2.15)$$

To construct both series y_t^t and y_t^p, we first identify an ARIMA model and then estimate its parameters. The model that best fits the output series is ARIMA(1,1,0). Examining the autocorrelation and partial autocorrelation functions of y_t, we find that the autocorrelations are very high for short lags and decay off gradually for longer lags. The partial autocorrelation for the first lag is close to one and for longer lags is quite small and sometime negative. This behavior is indicative of an integrated component. Furthermore, the behavior of autocorrelations and partial autocorrelations of the first difference confirmed a first order autoregressive model.

2.4.3 Expected Returns and Different Components of Output

The economic interpretation of the decomposed series has been extensively examined in the literature. For instance, Blanchard and Quah (1989) and Blanchard (1989) show that long run movements in output are primarily due to aggregate supply disturbances. These disturbances which include productivity shocks have a long term effect on output.[12] Short run movements in output, on the other hand, are due to aggregate demand disturbances that result from shocks to monetary and fiscal policy and are believed to have a transitory effect on output.

Given the significant economic difference in the information content of the permanent and the transitory components of output, it is important to examine the relationship between each of these components and expected stock returns. More specifically, which of these components contain more useful information with respect to predicting future stock returns? Using the permanent and transitory components as our state variables, the following regressions are estimated:

$$R_{t+1} = C_1 + \beta_1 Gy_t + e_{t+1} \qquad (2.16)$$

$$R_{t+1} = C_2 + \beta_2 Gy_t^p + \varepsilon_{t+1} \qquad (2.17)$$

$$R_{t+1} = C_3 + \beta_3 Gy_t^t + \eta_{t+1} \qquad (2.18)$$

where R_{t+1} is the real market return in period $t{+}1$ and Gy_t, Gy_t^p Gy_t^t are the rates of growth in the aggregate output, permanent component and transitory component of output respectively. The growth in the permanent component actually represents the sum of the innovations in the permanent component.[13]

Table 2.3 provides estimates for equations (2.16), (2.17) and (2.18) using rates of growth for the state variable measured over the previous three, six and twelve months respectively.[14] Panels A, B and C show the estimates of the parameters based on the value-weighted, equal-weighted and *S&P* 500 portfolios respectively.

Table 2.3: Univariate Regression Estimates of the Relation Between Expected Stock Returns and the Growth Rates of Different Components of Output

$$R_{t+1} = C + \beta(\text{State variable})_t + \varepsilon_{t+1}$$

Growth Rate	Panel A: VW CRSP		
	Gy_t	Gy_t^p	Gy_t^t
3-months	-1.07	-0.62	0.79
	(2.48)	(2.42)	(1.69)
	.052	.050	.025
6-months	-0.46	-0.39	0.64
	(1.84)	(2.15)	(1.72)
	.029	.040	.026
12-months	-0.32	-0.24	0.11
	(2.02)	(1.80)	(0.32)
	.035	.028	.001
	Panel B: EW CRSP		
3-months	-2.00	-1.71	1.51
	(3.10)	(3.05)	(2.13)
	.080	.077	.039
6-months	-0.87	-0.75	1.31
	(2.26)	(2.76)	(2.33)
	.044	.064	.046
12-months	-0.55	-0.43	0.33
	(2.32)	(2.18)	(0.63)
	.046	.041	.003
	Panel C: *S&P* 500		
3-months	-0.38	-0.23	0.24
	(1.66)	(1.45)	(0.65)
	.016	.012	.002
6-months	-0.22	-0.15	0.02
	(1.58)	(1.30)	(0.07)
	.014	.01	0
12-months	-0.25	-0.19	-0.03
	(2.84)	(2.45)	(0.12)
	.045	.034	0

The results in Table 2.3 point to several important findings. First, the negative relationship between expected stock returns and the growth rate in aggregate output appears to be robust regardless of the period of time over which the growth rate is calculated.

The second finding is more central to this study. The permanent component of output exhibits a negative and statistically significant relationship with expected stock returns. The predictive ability of the permanent component of output with respect to stock returns is similar to aggregate output and in some cases even better. This result implies that the predictability observed using aggregate output is in large part due to the permanent component of output.

The transitory component of output on the other hand, shows different results depending on the length of the interval over which the rate of growth is calculated. For rates of growth over three and six months, the transitory component appears to exhibit some explanatory power. It is interesting to observe that it has a positive relationship with expected stock returns. However since the transitory component is small in magnitude relative to the permanent component, it is not surprising that when the aggregate series is used to predict stock returns, we observe only the negative relationship. For growth rates calculated over twelve months, the significance of the transitory component disappears completely. The result is consistent with the notion that the transitory component represents short term fluctuations that are not likely to have any permanent effect on output.[15]

There are two other observations that are worth noting. When the output is used as the state variable as employed by BCM (1990), the estimates are more significant and exhibit a much higher R^2 than when rates of growth in output is used.[16] Furthermore, the estimates in Table 2.2 indicates that as we move from monthly to quarterly to annual frequency, we are likely to filter out the effect of the transitory component of output and hence obtain a more significant relationship between expected stock returns and the output variable. These findings provide an alternative explanation for the results obtained by Fama (1990) concerning the observed increase in the predictability of stock returns when longer term horizons are used.[17]

2.5 SUMMARY AND CONCLUSIONS

This chapter provides some new evidence regarding the justification of real industrial production as a predictor of stock returns. Specifically, instead of using aggregate output as the state variable, we decompose aggregate output into its permanent and transitory components. The permanent component is assumed to be affected by changes in the real factors in the economy such as capital accumulation, population growth and technological changes. The transitory component, on the other hand is assumed to be affected more by the monetary factors in the economy.

Our empirical results indicate that the permanent or growth component of output provides virtually all of the predictability attributed to the aggregate output variable. The transitory component of output however, appears to provide some useful information regarding the predictability of stock returns when the growth rate in output are calculated over short term horizons (three and six months). The usefulness of the transitory component in predicting stock returns appears to diminish in significance when growth rates are calculated over twelve months or longer periods. These results are indicative of a transitory component which represents only short term fluctuations that are not likely to have any permanent effect on output.

The theoretical appeal of these results is apparent. Capital accumulation, productivity increase and technological changes that are presumed to be the primary determinants to the shocks in the permanent component of output have long been recognized as important factors that affect the investment opportunity set (see Fama and Miller (1972)). On the other hand, monetary factors in the economy that result from fiscal and monetary disturbances are the primary determinants of the transitory component of output and are not supposed to be useful predictors of real stock returns.

These results are also consistent with general equilibrium pricing models in which firms are assumed to react in the next period to random productivity and technological shocks to the economy that occur in this period. Depending on the nature of the shock, firms divide their output between investment and dividends. Investors accordingly, adjust their incomes between savings and consumption. Invoking the consumption smoothing hypothesis by investors, a negative relationship between expected returns to investors and productivity shocks to the economy as reflected by the permanent component of output is established. No such relationship however, can be justified between expected returns and the shocks to the transitory component of output.

A fruitful area of research in the future might be to explore further the real factors that contribute to economic growth. For instance, a variable measuring technological changes or real shocks in the productivity of labor and capital might provide important insight into the relationship between macroeconomic variables and the returns on financial assets.

NOTES

1. This chapter appeared in the *Quarterly Review of Economics and Finance* and was coauthored with Dr. Hany Shawky.

2. This decomposition assumes that the aggregate output is affected by two kinds of shocks. One is permanent which results from increases in productivity, labor force etc. The other is transitory which may be caused by a bad crop, temporary increases or decreases in government spending or changes in the money supply. The permanent shock has a long term effect on output while the effect of a transitory shock on output is likely to disappear over time.

3. For further extensions and economic interpretations of the decomposed series, see Beveridge and Nelson (1981), Nelson and Plosser (1982) Campbell and Mankiw (1987), Cochrane (1988), Blanchard and Quah (1989) and Quah (1990).

4. For general equilibrium models also see Breeden (1986), Grossman and Shiller (1982), Cox, Ingersoll and Ross (1985) and Cochrane (1988).

5. While non-seasonally adjusted data is more consistent with theory, the use of seasonally adjusted industrial production growth rates does not appear to have a significant effect on the results. For instance, Fama (1990) uses seasonally adjusted data while BCM (1990) and Chen (1991) use seasonally unadjusted data with essentially the same conclusions.

6. To check for the stationarity of the output series, we examined the autocorrelation function and carried out Dickey-Fuller test of unit root (Dickey and Fuller 1981). For the aggregate output series, we could not reject the null hypothesis of unit root. For the rate of growth of output series however, we were able to accept the alternative hypothesis of no unit root.

7. As pointed out by Chen (1991), "the choice of measuring the rate of growth in output over the previous twelve months is somewhat arbitrary." In a subsequent section we examine the sensitivity of the results to alternative choices.

8. The use of '$\ln R_{t+1}$' in this regression is intended to provide a consistent comparison between the results using growth rates in output and those obtained by using trend in the output series as in BCM (1990). In subsequent regressions the '$\ln$' is dropped.

9. These results also indicate that the empirical relationship between aggregate output and expected stock returns is not sensitive to the unit root issue. In fact Cochrane (1988) pointed out that GNP can be characterized as an AR(2) about a deterministic trend or as a difference stationary ARMA process with a very small random walk component.

10. The fundamental difference between these two classes of non-stationary processes is that the difference stationary class is purely stochastic while the trend stationary class is essentially deterministic. By assuming that aggregate output is trend stationary, we are implicitly bounding uncertainty in the series and greatly restricting the relevance of the past to the future. For more details, see Nelson and Plosser (1982).

11. An alternative decomposition approach to the ARIMA representation is the unobserved component model. See Harvey and Todd (1983), Harvey (1985), Watson (1986) and Clark (1987).

12. Blanchard and Quah (1989) suggest that the effect of supply disturbances on output increases steadily over time, reaching a peak after two years and a plateau after five years. Demand disturbances on the other hand, reach a peak effect after one year and vanishes after two or three years.

13. It might seem inappropriate to consider growth rates for the transitory component. However, it should be noted that the short run effects on output represented by the transitory component could be as long as one year or even longer.

14. Using rates of growth over the previous 12 months as in Chen (1991) might obscure any relevant information due to short term fluctuations in the transitory component of output. Hence, we used shorter periods to calculate the growth rates.

15. Daniel and Torous (1993) found a negative contemporaneous relation between returns and the transitory component in its level form.

16. This behavior is typical of most macroeconomic series when used as regressors.

17. Specifically, Fama and French (1988) show that predictability of stock returns increases significantly for three to five years horizons.

CHAPTER 3

Expected Stock Returns and Volatility in Recessionary and Non-Recessionary Markets

3.1 INTRODUCTION

Rationalizing stock market volatility in the U.S. as well as other international equity markets remains an issue of concern to legislators, market participants and scholars in both finance and economics.[1] Inspite of the large body of empirical literature on the subject, some rather fundamental issues remain largely unresolved.[2] For instance, the source of market volatility and what causes it to fluctuate over time and whether in fact there is an appropriate level of volatility that is consistent with efficient markets are but a few of those issues.[3]

One important aspect of market volatility is how it relates to expected returns. For instance, Pindyck (1984) argues for a strong relationship between volatility and expected returns and attributes much of the decline in stock prices during the 1970's to increases in risk premia arising from increases in volatility. On the other hand, Poterba and Summers (1986), argue that the time-series properties of volatility do not support a strong relationship between volatility and expected risk premium.

French, Schwert and Stambaugh (1987) provide a direct test of the relationship between excess returns and volatility. They argue that a positive relationship between the expected risk premium and ex-ante volatility will induce a negative relationship between the excess holding period return and the unexpected change in volatility. Hence, combining the two components of volatility will obscure the ex-ante relation. As they observe a strong negative relationship between excess holding period returns and the unpredictable component of volatility, they interpret this result as indirect evidence of a positive relation between excess returns and ex-ante volatility.

This chapter examines the relationship between market volatility and excess stock returns using a two regime switching regression model. Given the evidence provided by Schwert (1989) that market volatility increases during recessionary time periods, it may be reasonable to expect that the structural relationship between market volatility and excess stock returns might also be significantly different in recessionary time periods than in non-recessionary market periods.

We find evidence of at least two regimes. Regime 1 is representative of "non-recessionary" market periods and is characterized by low variance. Regime 2 represents "recessionary" time periods and is characterized by a higher variance relative to regime 1.[4] For the non-recessionary market periods described by regime 1, we find no significant relationship between market volatility and excess returns while for regime 2, we find a highly significant negative relationship between market volatility and excess returns.

By decomposing volatility into its predictable and unpredictable components, we are able to show that in non-recessionary market periods, there is a positive and statistically significant relationship between excess returns and ex-ante market volatility. Furthermore, we show that the strong negative relationship between excess returns and the unpredictable component of volatility that was observed by French, Schwert and Stambaugh (1987) is only due to the recessionary market periods and does not represent the overall behavior of the market.

To further examine the robustness of our methodology we estimate the market price of risk using alternative proxies for the market portfolio. We shall argue that isolating recessionary periods from non-recessionary periods is also fundamental in estimating the market price of risk and is tantamount to Merton's (1980) approach which imposes a non-negativity constraint on the values of the market excess return parameter.

This chapter is organized in five sections. Section II describes the data and various proxies. Section III examines the relationship between market volatility and excess returns using a two regime switching regression model. Section IV presents estimates for the market price of risk using three alternative proxies for the market portfolio and a number of sample subperiods. The final section provides a brief summary and some concluding remarks.

3.2 DATA

The data used in this study consists of the daily returns series on the value-weighted and equal-weighted CRSP market portfolio and the S&P 500 composite portfolio, all obtained from the Center for Research in Security Prices (CRSP) for the period July 1962 through December 1990. The CRSP market portfolio contains all stocks listed on NYSE, AMEX and NASDAQ. The reason for using three different indices is to observe the sensitivity of the models estimated to the choice of the index. Yield on three-month treasury bills, obtained from the CITIBASE data was used as a proxy for the risk free interest rate. Daily stock returns were used to obtain continuously compounded monthly returns.

To identify the two market regimes we used the Business Cycle Indicators series 19 obtained from the Survey of Current Business. It is based on the monthly index of S&P 500 common stocks. Of the 342 months of data used in this study, 98 were identified as recessionary market periods and 244 as non-recessionary market periods. The specific dates for regimes one and two are given in the Table 3.1.

3.3 RELATIONSHIP BETWEEN RISK PREMIUM AND VOLATILITY IN A TWO REGIME MARKET

3.3.1 General Framework

A direct test of the relationship between the expected risk premium and market volatility can be expressed in the following form:

$$E\left(R_{mt} - R_{ft}\right) = \alpha + \beta\sigma_{mt} \qquad (3.1)$$

where R_{mt} is the monthly return on a stock market portfolio, R_{ft} is the monthly interest rate on the three-month treasury bills, σ_{mt} is the measure of the portfolio's monthly standard deviation. The monthly variance is calculated as the sum of the squared deviations of the daily non-overlapping returns from the sample mean i.e.

Table 3.1

This identifies the specific dates for regimes one and two. Essentially, the columns identified as "months duration" give the number of observations in each regime. The first column provides the specific calendar dates for both the regimes. For instance, the period from December 1961 to June 1962 is identified as a recessionary market period while the period from July 1962 to January 1966 is identified as a non-recessionary market period etc. Business Cycle Indicatior Series 19 has been used to determine the regimes.

Date of Cycle		Index Value		Months Duration		Percentage Change	
Peak	Trough	Peak	Trough	Rise	Decline	Rise	Decline
Dec 1961	Jun 1962	71.74	55.63	14	6	33.5	22.5
Jan 1966	Oct 1966	93.32	77.13	43	9	67.8	17.3
Dec 1968	Jun 1970	106.48	75.59	26	18	38.1	29.0
Jan 1973	Dec 1974	118.42	67.07	31	23	56.7	43.4
Sep 1976	Mar 1978	105.45	88.82	21	18	57.2	15.8
Feb 1980	Apr 1980	115.34	102.97	23	2	29.9	10.7
Nov 1980	Jul 1982	135.65	109.38	7	20	31.7	19.4
Aug 1987	Dec 1987	329.36	240.96	61	4	201.1	26.8
Jun 1990	Oct 1990	360.39	307.12	30	4	49.6	14.8

$$\sigma_{mt}^2 = \sum_{i=1}^{N_t}\left(R_{it} - \overline{R}_t\right)^2$$

where $\overline{R}_t$ is the sample mean of the daily market returns in month t. R_{it} is the daily market returns in month t. N_t is the number of trading days in a month.[5] If $\beta = 0$ in equation (3.1), the expected risk premium is unrelated to volatility. If $\beta > 0$, the expected risk premium is positively related to volatility and if $\beta < 0$, the expected risk premium is negatively related to volatility. Because the structural relationship described in equation (3.1) might change during recessionary time periods, we estimate a two regime switching regression model of the form:

$$E\left(R_{mt} - R_{ft}\right) = \alpha_1 + \beta_1\sigma_{mt} + \left(\alpha_2 - \alpha_1\right)D_t + \left(\beta_2 - \beta_1\right)\sigma_{mt}D_t + U_t \quad (3.2)$$

where

$$D_t = 0 \text{ for all } t \text{ identified as regime 1}$$

and

$$D_t = 1 \text{ for all } t \text{ identified as regime 2}$$

U_t satisfies all the basic conditions of a classical regression model. Two necessary conditions for using the switching regression model described by equation (3.2) is that; a) the variance of the error term in both regimes are the same and b) the switching points are known. Both conditions are satisfied in the present application.

Three alternative measures of volatility are estimated. The first measure is the monthly standard deviation which is calculated using the daily returns on the stock market portfolio within a given month. As pointed out by French, Schwert and Stambaugh (1987) this estimator has the advantage of more frequent sampling of the return process which increases the accuracy of the estimate. Furthemore, monthly estimates of the standard deviation using daily returns are more precise since we use returns only within that month. The other two measures of volatility are obtained by decomposing the monthly volatility estimates (standard deviation) into predictable and unpredictable components using autoregressive integrated moving average (ARIMA) models. The model that fits the value-weighted and equal-weighted portfolios volatility is ARIMA (2,0,0) and the model for the S&P 500 composite index is ARIMA (3,0,0). The fitted values of the regression represent the predictable component and the residuals represent the unpredictable component of volatility.

3.3.2 Risk Premium and Contemporaneous Volatility

Table 3.2 provide estimates for equation (3.1) and (3.2) using the S&P 500 composite portfolio, the value-weighted CRSP portfolio and the equal-weighted CRSP portfolio respectively. Panel A presents univariate regression estimates for the relationship between excess market returns and the contemporaneous standard deviation for the overall period while Panel B provides estimates for regime 1 and 2 separately.

The results in Table 3.2 provide consistent evidence for the relationship between excess market returns and volatility for all three market indices. For the overall period, (July 1962 through December 1990), the relationship between excess returns and standard deviations is reliably negative. This is a rather puzzling result. However, a plausible explanation of this negative relationship between excess returns and volatility emerges when the two market regimes are examined separately. In regime 2, this relationship is negative and highly significant whereas in regime 1, this relationship is not statistically significant.[6] It is quite clear however, that despite the relatively small number of sample observations (98) identified as regime 2, the negative relationship attributable to the recessionary market periods dominates the overall relationship when the estimates are obtained for the entire period.

These results strongly suggest that during recessionary time periods, when market volatility increases as was observed by Schwert (1989), realized stock returns are lower inducing a highly significant negative relationship between excess returns and contemporaneous volatility. As for the non-recessionary time periods represented as regime 1 in Table 3.2 Panel B, the data appears to provide no evidence of a significant relationship between excess market returns and contemporaneous market volatility.[7]

Table 3.2: Regression Estimates of the Relation Between Excess Stock Market Returns and Contemporaneous Volatility for the Period 1962-1990

$$R_{mt} - R_{ft} = C + \delta\sigma_{mt} + \eta_t$$

Panel A

Total Period	C	δ	R^2
S&P	.022	-.61	.115
	(5.83)	(6.52)	
VW	.012	-.277	.028
	(3.07)	(3.15)	
EW	.023	-.468	.045
	(4.72)	(4.01)	

$$R_{mt} - R_{ft} = \alpha_1 + \beta_1\sigma_{mt} + (\alpha_2 - \alpha_1)D_t + (\beta_2 - \beta_1)D_t + U_t$$

Panel B

		α	β	R^2
S&P	Regime 1	.012	-.027	.31
		(2.49)	(0.19)	
	Regime 2	.002	-.67	.31
		(0.40)	(6.26)	
VW	Regime 1	.012	.037	.20
		(3.15)	(0.41)	
	Regime 2	.01	-.95	.20
		(1.76)	(5.64)	
EW	Regime 1	.022	-.009	.20
		(4.41)	(0.07)	
	Regime 2	.03	-1.48	.20
		(3.28)	(6.68)	

3.3.3 Risk Premium and The Predictable and Unpredictable Components of Volatility

The predicted and unpredicted components of volatility are estimated using ARIMA models. Apparently, all portfolios have no integrated moving average term. S&P 500 follows an AR(3) process while value-weighted and equal-weighted portfolios follow an AR(2) process. The fitted value of the equation

$$\sigma_{mt} = p_1\sigma_{mt-1} + p_2\sigma_{mt-2} + \cdots + u_t$$

is used as the predicted component of volatility and the residual term ut as the unpredicted component of volatility. In this section, we examine the relationship between excess return and the predicted volatility using the following equation:

$$R_{mt} - R_{ft} = a + b\sigma_{mt}^p + e_t \qquad (3.3)$$

where σ_{mt}^p is the predicted component of volatility. For the relationship between excess returns and the unpredicted component of volatility we estimate the equation:

$$R_{mt} - R_{ft} = \theta + \gamma\sigma_{mt}^u + \zeta_t \qquad (3.4)$$

where σ_{mt}^u is the unpredicted component of volatility.

Tables 3.3 and Table 3.4 present the estimates for equation (3.3) and (3.4) which represents the relationship between excess returns and the predictable and unpredictable components of the standard deviation respectively. For the total period, we find a positive though statistically insignificant relation between excess returns and predicted volatility and a significant negative relationship between excess returns and the unpredictable component of volatility. These results are consistent with those found by French, Schwert and Stambaugh (1987).

Examining the results in Tables 3.3 and Table 3.4 for regime 1 and regime 2 market periods however, reveals a different story about the relationship between excess returns and volatility. In non-recessionary markets, there is a significant positive relationship between excess returns and the predictable component of volatility while in

Table 3.3: Regression Estimates of the Relation Between Excess Stock Market Returns and the Predictable Component of Volatility for the Period 1962-1990

$$R_{mt} - R_{ft} = \alpha + \beta \sigma_{mt}^{p} + e_{t}$$

Panel A

Total Period	α	β	R^2
S&P	.008	.05	.0002
	(1.19)	(0.29)	
VW	-.01	.556	.007
	(0.85)	(1.53)	
EW	-.02	1.16	.013
	(1.25)	(2.17)	

$$R_{mt} - R_{ft} = \alpha_1 + \beta_1 \sigma_{mt}^{p} + (\alpha_2 - \alpha_1) D_t + (\beta_2 - \beta_1) \sigma_{mt}^{p} D_t + U_t$$

Panel B

		α	β	R^2
S&P	Regime 1	-.01	.75	.26
		(1.86)	(3.41)	
	Regime 2	-.006	-.53	.26
		(0.66)	(2.29)	
VW	Regime 1	-.01	.82	.14
		(1.04)	(2.10)	
	Regime 2	-.05	.69	.14
		(2.00)	(1.01)	
EW	Regime 1	-.028	1.68	.12
		(1.57)	(2.85)	
	Regime 2	-.06	1.34	.12
		(1.90)	(1.26)	

Table 3.4: Regression Estimates of the Relation Between Excess Stock Market Returns and the Unpredictable Component of Volatility for the Period 1962-1990

$$R_{mt} - R_{ft} = \theta + \gamma\sigma_{mt}^u + \zeta_t$$

Panel A

Total Period	θ	γ	R^2
S&P	.006	-.79	.14
	(3.34)	(7.28)	
VW	.008	-.31	.034
	(3.23)	(3.47)	
EW	.014	-.54	.057
	(4.26)	(4.55)	

$$R_{mt} - R_{ft} = \alpha_1 + \beta_1\sigma_{mt}^u + (\alpha_2 - \alpha_1)D_t + (\beta_2 - \beta_1)\sigma_{mt}^u D_t + U_t$$

Panel B

		α	β	R^2
S&P	Regime 1	.01	-.61	.31
		(5.11)	(3.24)	
	Regime 2	-.02	-.67	.31
		(7.50)	(5.68)	
VW	Regime 1	.013	-.01	.23
		(5.01)	(0.13)	
	Regime 2	-.02	-1.17	.23
		(4.12)	(6.50)	
EW	Regime 1	.02	-.09	.22
		(5.81)	(0.77)	
	Regime 2	-.012	-1.66	.22
		(2.07)	(7.29)	

recessionary markets, there is no significant relationship between excess returns and the predictable component of volatility. Since the predictable component of volatility represents ex-ante volatility, our results indicate that only during non-recessionary market periods are the risk premiums positively related to ex-ante market volatility.

For the unpredictable component of volatility, we observe a negative and significant relationship between excess returns and the unpredicted volatility, but only in recessionary markets. The negative relation between excess returns and the unpredictable component of volatility observed by French, Schwert and Stambaugh (1987) for the overall period can best be explained by carefully examining Table 3.4. This negative relation is simply the result of the recessionary market period where only 28% of the sample observations are considered. For the much larger sample period identified as the non-recessionary market period (72% of the observations) such a negative relation between excess returns and the unpredictable component of volatility simply does not exist.

3.4 ESTIMATES OF THE MARKET PRICE OF RISK

3.4.1 Estimation Procedure

The slope of the capital market line represents the market price of risk for all efficient portfolios. Assuming that the market portfolio as measured by either of the three indices is an efficient portfolio, the appropriate measure for the market price of risk is given by

$$\left[\left(R_{mt} - R_{ft}/\sigma_{mt}\right)\right]$$

In this section we apply a number of alternative procedures to estimate the market price of risk. Essentially, we ask the following questions:

1. Can we obtain better estimates for the market price of risk by isolating recessionary and non-recessionary market periods?

2. How sensitive are the estimates to the time period considered?

3. How critical is the choice of the market index used?

4. How reasonable are the implied relative risk aversion coefficients based on three alternative market price of risk estimates?

Under certain conditions, Merton (1980) shows that in the context of an intertemporal equilibrium model, instantaneous expected excess return on the market can be reasonably approximated by:

$$E\left(R_{mt} - R_{ft}\right) = \lambda \sigma_{mt} \tag{3.5}$$

where λ is the slope of the capital market line or the market price of risk and is assumed to remain relatively stable for appreciable periods of time. All other variables are as defined before.

To estimate the market price of risk, Merton (1980) makes a strong argument for introducing a non-negativity constraint on the values of λ. Specifically, he argues that since realized market returns can be negative, it is certainly possible for λ to be negative for a particular time period. Can we then assume that the estimated λ is an unbiased measure of the true λ ? Given our prior knowledge that the expected excess return on the market must be positive, such a negative estimate of λ must be a biased low estimate of the true market price of risk. Thus a complete description of the model in equation (3.5) must include the condition that $\lambda > 0$. Merton (1980) incorporates this restriction by choosing a prior uniform distribution so that the prior density for λ is non-negative.

Instead of imposing a prior distribution on λ or on excess returns, we isolate estimates for non-recessionary and recessionary market periods. Since negative estimates of λ will often occur in recessionary market periods, estimating the market price of risk using only non-recessionary market periods is equivalent to Merton's non-negativity constraint on the values of λ.

3.4.2 Empirical Estimates

Using monthly observations for the period July 1962 through December 1990 we calculate the Sharpe ratio as a lower bound estimate for the market price of risk given in equation (3.5).[8] Estimates for the market price of risk for the entire sample period as well as for regime 1 and regime 2 market periods are provided in Table 3.5. The excess

Table 3.5: Estimates for the Market Price of Risk in Recessionary and Non-Recessionary Markets Using Monthly Data for the Period 1962-1990

$$\lambda = E\left(R_{mt} - R_{ft}\right)\big/\sigma_{mt}$$

Market period	R_{mt}	R_{ft}	σ_{mt}	λ
Panel A: S & P 500 Composite				
Total Period	.0061	.0056	.0353	.015
Regime 1	.0164	.0050	.0290	.393
Regime 2	-.0194	.0045	.0364	-.656
Panel B: Value-Weighted Portfolio				
Total Period	.0083	.0056	.0477	.056
Regime 1	.0189	.0050	.0406	.342
Regime 2	-.0172	.0045	.0536	-.405
Panel C: Equal-Weighted Portfolio				
Total Period	.0146	.0056	.0648	.138
Regime 1	.027	.0050	.0580	.379
Regime 2	-.0149	.0045	.0705	-.275

returns are calculated by subtracting the monthly mean risk free return from the mean market return and the standard deviation is calculated from the monthly return observations for that period. Three alternative proxies for the market portfolio are used to obtain three different estimates.

The results in Table 3.5 confirm our expectations and Merton's (1980) argument with respect to the likelihood of obtaining negative estimates for the market price of risk in some periods when excess market returns are negative. In this case, these periods are the recessionary market periods and including such observations is likely to bias the overall estimates downward. Furthermore, having argued that in non-recessionary market periods, realized returns are far more likely to match ex-ante returns, it follows that the market price of risk estimate obtained from regime 1 market data is more likely to be an unbiased estimate of the market participants' expectation of the market price of risk.

For the total period, the market price of risk estimates are inconsistent among different market proxies. For instance, using the

S&P 500 composite portfolio, the estimate is as low as 0.015 while for the equal-weighted CRSP portfolio, the estimate is 0.138. These estimates while arguably low are similar to those obtained by Bekaert and Hodrick (1992), French, Schwert and Stambaugh (1987), Friend and Blume (1975), Hansen and Singleton (1982) and Brown and Singleton (1985).

The market price of risk estimates for the non-recessionary market periods are consistent under the three alternative market proxies. The estimates for the three portfolios are 0.393, 0.342 and 0.379 giving a mean estimate for the market price of risk of 0.371. Interestingly, Merton (1980) provides an estimate of 0.3719 for the market price of risk using the non-negativity constraint on the values of λ.

The implied estimates for the relative risk aversion coefficient corresponding to the non-recessionary period market price of risk estimates in Table 3.5 are 13.55, 8.42 and 6.53 for the S&P, value-weighted and equal-weighted portfolios respectively. This gives a mean relative risk aversion (RRA) coefficient of 9.5. Merton (1980) finds a comparable estimate of 8.5.

Table 3.6: Price of Risk Estimates for Various Subperiods Using Data for the Period 1962-1990

Period	N	S&P	VW	EW
4 Year Subperiods				
1963-1966	48	.103	.115	.26
1967-1970	48	-.058	.04	.146
1971-1974	48	-.26	-.18	-.13
1975-1978	48	.091	.176	.36
1979-1982	48	-.027	.06	.195
1983-1986	48	.21	.192	.202
1987-1990	48	.108	.038	.011
Average		.024	.063	.149
14 Year Subperiods				
1962-1976	174	.0069	.041	.135
1977-1990	168	.0386	.077	.153
Average		.022	.059	.144
28 Year Period				
1962-1990	342	.015	.056	.138

Table 3.7: Price of Risk Estimates for Various Subperiods Using Non-Recessionary Market Data Over the Period 1962-1990

$$\lambda = E\left(R_{mt} - R_{ft}\right)\big/\sigma_{mt}$$

Period	N	S & P	VW	EW
4 Year Subperiods				
1963-1966	39	.465	.391	.563
1967-1970	30	.411	.498	.697
1971-1974	25	.288	.235	.159
1975-1978	29	.334	.315	.371
1979-1982	26	.618	.599	.72
1983-1986	48	.210	.192	.202
1987-1990	40	.568	.312	.352
Average		.413	.363	.437
14 Year Subperiods				
1962-1976	122	.407	.352	.413
1977-1990	122	.370	.309	.346
Average		.388	.330	.379
28 Year Period				
1962-1990	244	.393	.342	.379

To examine the consistency of these estimates, we compute the market price of risk for seven 4-year subperiods and two 14-year subperiods. Table 3.6 present the market price of risk estimates when all the data is considered while Table 3.7 provides the estimates for non-recessionary market periods only.

For the overall period, the estimates are again quite low and different for the three indices. However, for the estimates obtained using the non-recessionary market periods only, Table 3.7 provides consistent values for the market price of risk across the three indices. In addition, the values for the market price of risk for the non-recessionary market periods computed using 4-year subperiods and 14-year subperiods produce relatively similar results for the market price of risk computed over the entire 28-year period. A grand mean for all nine estimates obtained in Table 3.7 gives a market price of risk of 0.38.

3.5 SUMMARY AND CONCLUSIONS

This chapter examines the relationship between market volatility and excess returns for a two regime market for the period July 1962 through December 1990. Using monthly observations and three alternative proxies for the market portfolio, the major findings of this study can be summarized as follows:

1. There is a highly significant negative relationship between excess returns and market volatility during recessionary market periods that tends to dominate the overall relationship. Removing recessionary market periods from the data, we find no significant relationship between excess market returns and the contemporaneous measure of market volatility.

2. Decomposing volatility into its predictable and unpredictable components however, we find that in non-recessionary market periods, there is a positive and statistically significant relationship between excess returns and ex-ante market volatility. Furthermore, we show that the strong negative relationship between excess returns and the unpredictable component of volatility holds only in recessionary market periods and is not an appropriate characterization for the overall behavior of the market.

3. Estimating the market price of risk using non-recessionary market periods is shown to be equivalent to Merton's (1980) approach which imposes a non-negativity constraint on the prior distribution of the market price of risk estimates. We estimate the market price of risk to be between .36 and .40 for the period 1962-1990.

4. Inspite of the significant differences in the mean and variances of the three market portfolio proxies examined, the above conclusions remain unchanged for the three indices.

NOTES

1. This chapter was published in *The Journal of Economics and Business* which was jointly written with Dr. Hany Shawky.

2. Important work in this area include Officer (1973), Shiller (1979, 1981a, 1981b), Grossman and Shiller (1981), Flavin (1983), Mankiw, Romer and Shapiro (1985) and more recently Poterba and Summers (1986), West

(1988), Schwert (1989) and LeRoy and Parke (1992). In an international context, see Bekaert and Hodrick (1992), Campbell and Hamao (1992) and Roll (1992).

3. For an interesting discussion of these issues, see presentations by J. Tobin, W. Gramm, M. Sato, S. Timbers, M. Miller, R. Shiller, and R. Roll in a Symposium on "Volatility in U.S. and Japanese Stock Markets", Journal of Applied Corporate Finance, Spring 1992.

4. For an estimate of variance in recessionary versus non-recessionary market periods, see Table 3.1.

5. We do not correct for autocorrelation in the daily returns. French, Schwert and Stambaugh (1987) show that such a correction does not have any significant effect on the resulting estimates.

6. As pointed out by Cadsby (1992) and many others, the fact that statistical investigations cannot find a significantly positive relationship between risk and return during periods when market returns are low or negative is consistent with the CAPM. For instance, high beta stocks should do particularly bad during periods when market returns are negative because that is precisely what "high beta" means.

7. As will be shown in a subsequent section, it is the predicted or the ex-ante volatility that is found to be significantly positively related to excess returns.

8. Bekaert and Hodrick (1992) extend the work of Hansen and Jagannathan (1991) by deriving a bound that restricts the coefficient of variation of the nominal intertemporal marginal rate of substitution (Market price of risk) to be greater than or equal to the Sharpe ratio of excess returns.

CHAPTER 4

Stock Market Bubbles
Some Historical Perspective

4.1 INTRODUCTION

In this chapter we examine peak to peak percentage changes in the S&P composite stock price index involving new historic highs which are separated by cumulative declines amounting to three percent or more.[1]

The objective of this study is to provide some historical perspective and also test the efficient market hypothesis by examining economic and financial environments or conditions that might enable one to do a better job of discriminating between small and large "bubbles" and between bubbles that are separated by relatively small "corrections" and major stock market crashes. If the percentage changes in the S&P index from one bubble peak to the next are sufficiently small, on the average, one can expect modest trading profits from a simple strategy of selling a portfolio similar to the S&P index after it has recovered to a new historic high and repurchasing the index after the next cumulative decline amounting to three percent or more. At that point one would really like to be able to determine whether the decline in stock prices is likely to be a minor correction or the beginning of a major bear market.

4.2 BULL MARKETS IN PERSPECTIVE

Since the S&P index was first computed on a daily basis in 1928 there have so far been eleven occasions when it lost 13.9% or more of its value after climbing to a new historic high. After the S&P index finally recovered from these major bear markets and achieved at least one more new historic high there have always been at least three minor declines or corrections of from three to 10.6% (followed by a recovery to yet another new historic high) before the stock market entered a more pronounced bear market of greater severity. See column (4) of Table 4.1.

Five of the eleven bull markets with new historic highs for the S&P index in the post World War II period ended on the fourth decline of three percent or more and two bull markets on the fifth decline. In 1996 the US stock market finally broke the 1985-87 bull market record of 12 minor peak to trough declines of from three to 9.4% before a major crash. The worst decline during the longer lasting bull market of 1991-97 has so far only amounted 8.9% from February 2, 1994 to April 11 of the same year.

The most impressive aspect to the bull market of 1991-95 is its subdued character prior to the record setting peak to peak gain of 29 % during 1995. The bubble which peaked out on February 2, 1994 established a new all time first peak to last peak trading day duration record of 116 days but only increased a modest 5.63% above the preceding new high bubble peak which occurred on March 10, 1993.

On December 13, 1995 this record was broken with a series of 77 new historic highs for the S&P composite spread over a 210 day trading period without a correction of three percent or more. The 29% peak-to-peak gain associated with this bubble was more than ten percentage points higher than the previous record of 18.8% which was established during the bull market of 1985-87.

The 1991-96 bull market has already established another new all time duration record of more than six years from its first new high on February 13, 1991. The previous record for a new high bull market without a correction amounting to 13.9% or more was only about 2 and 2/3 years from January 21, 1985 to August 25, 1987.

It is not easy to predict the demise of a bull market. The data in Table 4.1 would suggest, however, that bull markets are more likely to end after a relatively small peak-to-peak gain in column (3) than after a spectacular series of new historic highs that have been achieved without an intervening decline amounting to three percent or more. There have so far only been two cases—the bull markets of 1967-68 and 1980 where the last peak to peak gain in stock prices was the largest bubble in that bull market.

Table 4.1 Declines of Three Percent or More in the S&P 500 Stock Price Index After it Has Achieved a New All Time High Since September 7, 1929

Date of		Value S&P		% Change S&P: Peak To		Trading Day
Peak	Trough	Peak (1)	Trough (2)	Peak (3)	Trough (4)	Duration (5)n
9/ 7/29	6/ 1/32	31.92	4.40**	—	-86.2	
10/ 6/54	10/29/54	32.76	31.68	2.6	-3.3	10
1/ 3/55	1/17/55	36.75	34.58	12.2$	-5.9ϕ	40H
3/ 4/55	3/14/55	37.52	34.96	2.1$	-6.8	19
4/21/55	5/17/55	38.32*	36.97	2.1	-3.5	7
7/27/55	8/10/55	43.76	41.74	14.2	-4.6ϕ	37
9/23/55	10/11/55	45.63	40.80	4.3	-10.6	13
11/14/55	1/23/56	46.41	43.11	1.7$	-7.1	0
3/20/56	5/28/56	48.87	44.10	5.3$	-9.8	7
8/ 2/56	10/22/57	49.74	38.98**	1.8	-21.6	13
11/17/58	11/25/58	53.24	51.02	7.0	-4.2ϕ	37
1/21/59	2/ 9/59	56.04	53.58	5.3$	-4.4ϕ	27
5/29/59	6/10/59	58.68	56.36	4.7	-4.0ϕ	61H
8/ 3/59	10/25/60	60.71*	52.30**	3.5	-13.9	22
4/17/61	4/24/61	66.68	64.40	9.8	-3.4ϕ	54H
5/17/61	7/18/61	67.39E	64.41D	1.1	-4.4	2
9/ 6/61	9/25/61	68.46E	65.77D	1.6	-3.9	22

Table 4.1 (continued)

| Date of | | Value S&P | | % Change S&P: Peak To | | Trading Day |
Peak	Trough	Peak (1)	Trough (2)	Peak (3)	Trough (4)	Duration (5)n
12/12/61	6/26/62	72.64E*	52.32D**	6.1	-28.0	35
10/28/63	11/22/63	74.48	69.61	2.5	-6.5	39
5/12/64	6/ 8/64	81.16	78.64	9.0	-3.1φ	101H
7/17/64	8/26/64	84.01	81.32	3.5	-3.2φ	15
11/20/64	12/15/64	86.28*	83.22	2.7	-3.5	17
5/13/65	6/28/65	90.27	81.60	4.6	-9.6	81
2/ 9/66	10/ 7/66	94.06	73.20**	4.2	-22.2	94
5/ 8/67	6/ 5/67	94.58	88.43	.6	-6.5	2
8/ 4/67	8/28/67	95.83	92.64	1.3	-3.3	4
9/25/67	3/ 5/68	97.59	87.72	1.8$	-10.1	8
7/11/68	8/ 2/68	102.39*	96.63	4.9	-5.6	44H
11/29/68	5/26/70	108.37	69.29**	5.8	-36.1	38
4/12/72	5/ 9/72	110.18	104.74D	1.7	-4.9	24
5/26/72	7/20/72	110.66	105.81D	.4	-4.4	2
8/14/72	10/16/72	112.55	106.77D	1.7	-5.1	4
12/11/72	12/21/72	119.12*	115.11D	5.8	-3.4φ	26H
1/11/73P	10/ 3/74	120.24	62.28D**	.9	-48.2	6
8/22/80P	8/28/80	126.02	122.08	4.8$	-3.1φ	26H

Table 4.1 (continued)

| Date of | | Value S&P | | % Change S&P: Peak To | | Trading Day |
Peak	Trough	Peak (1)	Trough (2)	Peak (3)	Trough (4)	Duration (5)n
9/22/80P	9/29/80	130.40	123.54	3.5$	-5.3	13
10/15/80P	10/30/80	133.70	126.29	2.5$	-5.5	7
11/28/80P	8/12/82	140.52*	102.42**	5.1$	-27.1	11
11/ 9/82	11/23/82	143.02	132.93	1.8$	-7.1	4
1/10/83	1/24/83	146.78	139.97	2.6$	-4.6	2
6/22/83	8/ 8/83	170.99	159.18	16.5	-6.9φ	94H
10/10/83	7/24/84	172.65*	147.82**	1.0$	-14.4	0
2/13/85	3/15/85	183.35	176.53	6.2$	-3.7φ	17
6/ 6/85	6/13/85	191.06	185.33	4.2	-3.0φ	29
7/17/85	9/25/85	195.65	180.66	2.4	-7.7	13
1/ 7/86	1/22/86	213.80*	203.49	9.3$	-4.8φ	37
3/27/86	4/ 7/86	238.97	228.63	11.8	-4.3φ	37
4/21/86	5/16/86	244.74	232.76	2.4$	-4.9	3
5/29/86	6/10/86	247.98	239.58	1.3$	-3.4	2
7/ 2/86	7/15/86	252.70	233.66	1.9	-7.5	5
9/ 4/86	9/29/86	253.83	229.91	.4$	-9.4	6
12/ 2/86	12/31/86	254.00	242.17	.1$	-4.7	0
3/24/87	3/30/87	301.64	289.20	18.8	-4.1φ	53H
4/ 6/87	5/20/87	301.95	278.21D	.1	-7.9	0

Table 4.1 (continued)

Date of		Value S&P		% Change S&P: Peak To		Trading Day
Peak	Trough	Peak (1)	Trough (2)	Peak (3)	Trough (4)	Duration (5)n
8/25/87	12/ 4/87	336.77	223.92**	11.5	-33.5	50
9/ 1/89	9/14/89	353.73	343.16	5.0$	-3.0φ	27H
10/ 9/89	1/30/90	359.80	322.98	1.7$	-10.2	4
6/ 4/90P	6/26/90	367.40	352.06	2.1$	-4.2	4
7/16/90P	10/11/90	368.95*	295.46**	.4	-19.9	0
4/17/91	5/15/91	390.45	368.57	5.8	-5.6φ	43
8/ 6/91	8/19/91	390.62	376.47	.0$	-3.6	0
8/28/91	10/ 9/91	396.64	376.80	1.5	-5.0	4
11/13/91	11/29/91	397.41E*	375.22	.2	-5.6	1
1/15/92	4/ 8/92	420.77E	394.50	5.9	-6.2	14
8/ 3/92	8/24/92	425.09E	410.72	1.0$	-3.4	3
9/14/92	10/ 9/92	425.27E	402.66D	.0$	-5.3	0
2/ 4/93	2/18/93	449.56E	431.90	5.7	-3.9φ	51
3/10/93	4/26/93	456.33E	433.54D	1.55$	-5.0	2
2/ 2/94	4/ 4/94	482.00E	438.92D	5.6	-8.9	116
12/13/95	1/10/96	621.69	598.48D	29.0	-3.7φ	210H
2/12/96	4/11/96	661.45	631.18D	6.4	-4.6φ	10
5/24/96	7/24/96	678.51	626.65D	2.6$	-7.6	9
11/18/96	12/16/96	757.03	720.98D	11.6G$	-4.8φ	51

Table 4.1 (continued)

Date of		Value S&P		% Change S&P: Peak To		Trading Day
Peak	Trough	Peak (1)	Trough (2)	Peak (3)	Trough (4)	Duration (5)n
2/18/97	4/11/97	816.29	737.65D	7.8G	-9.6	26
8/6/97	8/29/97	960.32	899.47	17.6$	-6.3φ	65
10/7/97	10/27/97	983.12	876.99	2.4	-10.8	3
12/5/97	1/09/98	983.79	927.69	0.1$	-5.7	0

(5)n. Number of additional trading days after the recovery to a first new high to the last new high or peak date.

* Fourth new high to be followed by a three percent decline for the bull market in question.

** A major bear market low.

$ identifies cases where the first new high was associated with a daily gainof 1.1% or more.

φ Cases where the peak to trough decline in column (4) is less than the preceding peak to peak increase in column (3).

D identifies cases where the first new high occurred after a month when the dividend yield for the S&P index was equal to 3.0% or less.

E identifies cases where the first new high occurred after a quarter when the P/E ratio for the S&P index was equal to 20.50 or more.

G identifies peak to peak gains that may have encouraged Fed Chairman Alan Greenspan to warn investors about the possibility of irrational exuberance.

H identifies the trading day duration record, without a cumulative decline of three percent or more, for each bull market separated by cumulative declines of 13% or more.

P identifies declines of three percent or more that occurred during years containing a recessionary peak designated by the National Bureau of Economic Research.

Source of basic data: The Practical Forecasters' Almanac(Burr Ridge, Illinois: Irwin, 1992), Table 3.05 and Standard and Poor's Security Price Index Record. %

Table 4.2: The Sell and Repurchase Values for the S&P Composite Stock Price Index Associated with a Strategy of Selling the Index after a First New Historic High—if the Preceding Month's Dividend Yield Was Equal to 3.0% or Less—and Repurchasing It after the Next Cumulative Decline of Three Percent or More.

Sell Date	Buy Date	Div. Yield Previous Month (1)	P/E Ratio Previous Quarter (2)	S&P Closing Values on		% Change S&P Index (5)
				Sell Date (3)	Buy Date (4)	
5/15/61	6/16/61	2.95	21.1	66.83	65.18	-2.5
8/04/61	9/25/61	3.00	21.3	67.68	65.77	-2.8
10/20/61	1/05/62	2.93	21.9	68.48	69.66	1.7
3/06/72	5/01/72	2.92	17.9	108.77	106.69	-1.9*
5/24/72	6/08/72	2.83	18.5	110.31	107.28	-2.7
8/08/72	9/12/72	2.90	18.0	110.69	108.47	-2.0*
11/01/72	12/21/72	2.82	18.0	112.67	115.11	2.2*
1/03/73	1/26/73	2.70	18.4	119.57	116.45	-2.6
4/06/87	4/09/87	2.90	19.3	301.95	292.86	-3.0
9/14/92	10/02/92	2.97	23.9	425.27	410.47	-3.5
3/08/93	4/02/93	2.81	22.8	454.71	441.39	-2.9
8/19/93	2/24/94	2.81	22.3	456.43	464.26	1.7
2/14/95	1/10/96	2.87	15.0	482.55	598.48	24.0*
1/29/96	2/29/96	2.30	18.1	624.22	640.43	2.6*
5/13/96	7/05/96	2.24	19.0	661.51	657.44	-.6
9/13/96	12/12/96	2.22	19.2	680.54	729.82	7.2
1/10/97	2/28/97	2.01	19.1	759.50	790.82	4.1

*Percentage change in the S&P index when the P/E ratio in the previous quarter in column (2) was less than 18.4.

Further evidence in support of the conclusion that new high bull markets usually don't end abruptly can be inferred from the number of trading days shown in column (5) which have supported the new high portion of each bubble. None of the major bull markets in Table 4.1 have (so far) ended after the record number of trading days (for the most enduring bubble in that particular bull market) without a cumulative decline of three percent or more. The tendency for major bull markets to "fade away" instead of ending on a big bubble, or a spectacular series of new historic highs, makes it far more difficult to define an optimal trend chasing strategy than to compute the profits which "might have been obtained" as a result of simpler policies of "buying low and selling high".

4.3 A TRADING STRATEGY BASED ON STOCK MARKET VOLATILITY

When the average percentage gain from one bubble peak to the next bubble peak in column (3) of Table 4.1 is less than, or not very much greater than three percent, it will be profitable, on the average, for a tax exempt investor in a no load mutual fund similar to the S&P index to liquidate his or her portfolio at the end of the day the S&P index first recovers to a new high (after experiencing a cumulative dip of three percent or more), put the proceeds in a money market fund, and stay out of the equity market until the end of the day the S&P index has again experienced a cumulative decline amounting to at least three percent.

On March 8, 1993, for example, the S&P index closed at a new historic high of 454.71 after recovering from a cumulative dip amounting to about 3.9% following the preceding new high peak of 449.56 which had occurred on February 4. Selling a portfolio similar to the S&P index on March 8 would have been a bit premature since the index achieved another new high of 456.33 on March 10. The S&P index then proceeded to drift lower. On April 2 it lost 8.91 points and closed at 441.39. At that closing value the S&P index was down 3.3% from the last new high peak on March 10 and was about 2.9% lower than our assumed selling price of 454.71 on March 8. The repurchase discount of 2.9% from a strategy of transacting at end of the day closing prices, in this example, is about twice as great as the discount that could have been obtained from an open order strategy of selling the S&P index when it first equaled the peak value for the preceding bubble and repurchasing after a cumulative decline of exactly three percent.

From this example it should be clear that one really needs more information than is actually provided in Table 4.1 to compute the gains and losses associated with an end of the day trading strategy. The additional information is provided in Tables 4.2 and 4.3 for two trading strategies.

It is interesting, in any event, to try to determine what kinds of economic and financial environments are likely to create the caution and anxiety that will produce small bubbles (or percentage gains from one bubble peak to the next bubble peak) and make it worth while to get out of the market, on the average, or at least refrain from buying a portfolio similar to the S&P index after it has recovered from a cumulative decline of three percent or more and achieved a new historic high.

Devising a trading strategy of this type that will outperform a policy of buy and hold is not an easy matter. An investor who exited the market after every first new high and repurchased the S&P index after the first cumulative dip of three percent would have experienced a lot of ups and down and gone almost no where from September 22, 1954 to February 14, 1995. The investor's net gain, before taxes and transaction costs, would have only been a paltry 6.6% compared to a more spectacular gain of 1408.0% for a policy of buy and hold.

While most investors are probably well advised to ignore market timing approaches to stock market participation, there are a few trading strategies that would have outperformed buy and hold—if we ignore taxes and transaction costs. One hypothesis, which was advanced by Renshaw in (1991) is that new high trading strategies work best in a volatile market. Greater volatility, other things equal, will produce more end of the day breakage above the preceding bubble peak and below the minimum decline required for repurchase. In so doing it will accentuate the gain to be expected from an asymmetric relationship between percentage gains and losses. A three percent decline from say 100 to 97, for example, requires a recovery of a little over 3.09 % just to get back to 100.

One indicator of stock market volatility is the percentage gain in the S&P index the day it first recovers to a new historic high. For the 27 cases from 9/7/29 to 7/5/96, when the first daily recovery gain to a new historic high was equal to 1.1% or more, it would have been possible (for a tax exempt investor with no transaction costs) to obtain 46.6%

more price appreciation, than under a policy of buy and hold, by selling a portfolio similar to the S&P at the end of that day and repurchasing the portfolio at the end of the day the S&P index first experienced another cumulative new high decline amounting to three percent or more.

An investor who followed this trading strategy by selling a portfolio similar to the S&P index on September 14, 1996—after the new high recovery from the nerve racking correction of 7.6% from May 24 to July 24— would have suffered a loss of 7.2% or more compared to a policy of "buy and hold". The exuberant bull market of 1995-97, in any event, has ruined a lot of market timing strategies.

The 1.1% or more gain required on the first recovery day to measure volatility and trigger a sale was chosen in an attempt to maximize the cumulative advantage to be obtained from this type of "three percent" switching strategy. See those peak to peak gains in column (3) of Table 4.1 which are identified with a $ sign.

Most of the more profitable volatility switches involving a first new high daily gain of 1.1% or more have occurred since the invention of stock index futures and options in 1982. These innovations have made it easier and more profitable for traders and speculators to "short" an over valued market. Lots of volatility associated with the first four bubbles in a bull market may be indicative of a near term crash. The three bull markets with three or more dollar signs attached to the first four bubbles (the 1980, 1982-83 and 1989-90 bull markets) all ended on the bursting of the fourth bubble.

4.4 BUBBLE SIZE IN RELATION TO EARNINGS AND DIVIDENDS

There are a number of other environments where modest profits could have been obtained, on the average, by employing a three percent or more switching strategy. One of the most publicized indicators of an "over valued market" is a dividend yield for the S&P index of three percent or less (Renshaw 1990 and 1992). This indicator, however, has not worked very well in recent years. See Table 4.2.

The poor performance of a low dividend yield exit strategy, by itself, during the bull market of 1995, however, makes it clear that traders should also keep a close eye on what is happening to earnings. From the fourth quarter of 1993 to the fourth quarter of 1994 the

Table 4.3: The Sell and Repurchase Values for the S&P Composite Stock Price Index Associated with a Strategy of Selling the Index after a First New Historic High—if the Preceding End of the Quarter P/E Ratio Was Over 20.50— and Repurchasing It after the Next Cumulative Decline of Three Percent or More.

Sell Date	Buy Date	P/E Ratio Previous Quarter (1)	S&P Closing Values on		% Change S&P Index (4)
			Sell Date (2)	Buy Date (3)	
5/15/61	6/16/61	21.1	66.83	65.18	-2.5*
8/04/61	9/25/61	21.3	67.68	65.77	-2.8*
10/20/61	1/05/62	21.9	68.48	69.66	1.7*
11/12/91	11/15/91	21.8	396.74	382.62	-3.6
12/24/91	2/18/92	21.8	399.33	407.38	2.0
7/29/92	8/24/92	23.9	422.23	410.72	-2.7
9/14/92	10/02/92	23.9	425.27	410.47	-3.5*
11/20/92	2/16/92	22.2	426.65	433.91	1.7
3/08/93	4/02/93	22.8	454.71	441.39	-2.9*
8/19/93	2/24/94	23.3	456.43	464.26	1.7*
7/1/97	8/12/97	21.8	891.03	926.53	3.9
{Average % Change from Sell Date to Buy Date}					-1.34

*Identifies cases where the dividend yield in the preceding month was equal to three percent or less. The average decline associated with these six cases is 1.38%.

quarterly earnings associated with the *S&P* index increased 65.3%. This was the largest fourth quarter to fourth quarter increase in corporate earnings since 1946. The explosive increase in earnings helped to lower the P/E ratio from 21.3 at the end of 1993 to a more normal 15.0 at the end of 1994. The expectation that earnings would continue to increase at a rapid rate set the stage for one of the most remarkable bubbles in stock market history.

In a world where it has become fashionable for many corporations to use their earnings to buy up other companies, or repurchase their own stock, it is reasonable to suppose that high price/earnings ratios may be a more reliable indication of overvaluation than low dividend yields. For the ten cases where the P/E ratio for the S&P index at the end of the preceding quarter was in excess of 20.50 one could have obtained eleven percent more price appreciation with a first new high sale and buy back strategy after the next decline of three percent, than under a buy and hold policy.

A crash indicator threshold of 20.50 for the P/E ratio was first proposed by Renshaw in (1990). Since then we have had seven additional out of sample cases of new high bubbles following a P/E ratio in excess of this threshold. The average discount to be obtained from exiting the market after a P/E ratio of 20.50 or more is enhanced somewhat, however, if one only considers the six cases where the dividend yield was equal to 3.0% or less.

4.5 LARGE CORRECTIONS

The most severe "correction" in Table 4.1 is the 10.6% decline in the S&P index from September 23 to October 11, 1955 which contained a one day drop in stock prices amounting to 6.6% on September 26, following President Eisenhower's heart attack.

There have been eight large corrections in major bull markets involving declines of from 7.9% to 10.6%. For the seven resolved cases an investor could have always sold a portfolio similar to the S&P index after the first day of recovery to a new historic high and then repurchased the same portfolio at a discount of at least 11.8% during the next stock market crash.

Whether mega buck profits from this kind of trading strategy will continue to occur in the future is one of the more interesting questions to be resolved with the passage of time. While the goal of most market timers is to avoid large corrections and market crashes, the out of sample history of crash indicators that would have produced large trading profits in the past is not very encouraging (Renshaw, 1995a).

One reason for at least hoping that the rather spectacular bubble which emerged after the 8.9% correction of 1994 won't be followed by an horrendous crash, is evidence suggesting that the stock market is more stable now than it used to be (Renshaw 1995b). The three smallest annual high/low ratios for the S&P index were all recorded in the 1992-94 period. There is also the prolonged nature of the 1991-96 new high bull market which suggests that stock market crashes in the midst of prosperity may not be occurring as frequently as was the case during the 1960s, 70s and 80s.

4.6 STOCK MARKET CRASHES IN THE MIDST OF PROSPERITY

Four of the ten completed new high bull markets in Table 4.1 ended as a result of stock market crashes in the midst of prosperity. All of these crashes (the debacles of 1962, 1966, 1984 and 1987) were preceded by at least one new high, peak-to-peak gain of nine percent or more for the S&P index in column 3 of Table 4.1. This is the only characteristic of new high bull markets terminated by bear markets in the midst of prosperity (that we have discovered) that is not widely shared by the six (completed) new high bull markets which were terminated by recessions. The implication would seem to be that crashes in the midst of prosperity can be explained, at least in part, by "excessive" optimism or speculative enthusiasm.

In the post World War II period there have been only eleven new high peak to peak gains in column (3) of Table 4.1 amounting to nine percent or more. Seven of these bubbles "broke" during quarters when the annualized growth of real GDP in 1987 dollars was over five percent or during quarters when the four quarter growth rate for real GDP was in excess of five percent.

Two of these cases occurred in 1987, before the October crash, when the economic growth rate had slowed to a more normal pace and the stock market was still imbued with a tremendous amount speculative enthusiasm. The largest bubble of all broke during the fourth quarter of 1995 after real GDP for the third quarter expressed in chain weighted dollars had increased at an annualized rate of 3.6 after increases of only 0.6% and 0.5% for the first two quarters.

It should be noted, however, that only one of these large new high bubbles, the 11.5% increase in stock prices from June 15, 1987 to August 25, was followed by a crash. The other nine bubbles only experienced minor corrections or declines ranging from a loss of 3.1% for the 1964 bubble to a loss of 6.9% for the 1983 bubble.

4.7 THE POSSIBILITY OF ANOTHER RECESSION

If one could have accurately anticipated years containing a recessionary peak in business activity that information would have been of considerable value in avoiding financial loss.

There have so far only been seven new high bubbles in the post 1953 period that occurred during years containing a recessionary peak in business activity. See those peak dates identified with a "P" in Table 4.1. Investors who exited the market in these years after the first new high and repurchased a portfolio similar the S&P after a closing dip of three percent or more could have obtained an average trading profit (before taxes and commissions) of 1.34%.

Larger gains could have been achieved by simply staying out of the market until it was clear that the US economy had slipped into another recession. Since the mild recession of 1960-61 the S&P composite stock price index has consistently lost more of its value, measured on a monthly average basis, after a recessionary peak in business activity as defined by the National Bureau of Economic Research than before the peak.

The duration of business expansions has been increasing with the passage of time. The five business expansions from 1961-90 had an average duration of 60.8 months. This can be compared to an average duration of only 36.2 months for the first four expansions after World War II and an average duration of only 29 months for the 22 expansions from 1854-1945.

One of the problems that nervous investors face in relation to the business cycle is that economists have not had very much success at identifying recessionary peaks in business activity in close proximity to their occurrence (Siegel, 1994, p. 180).

There is a time honored rule of thumb that a recession will soon follow three consecutive declines in the Conference Board's index of leading economic indicators. The lead times for this signal, however, have ranged from only two months for the recessions of 1948-49 and

1953-54 to a grand total of 90 months for the three declines which occurred during the stock market crash of 1962.

In thinking about the possibility of a near term peak in business activity it should be appreciated that modern day recessions are not as severe as they used to be. During the recession of 1948-49, payroll employment declined by 5.2% and industrial production by ten percent. During the 1990-91 recession payroll employment experienced a dip of only 1.7% and industrial production only declined 4.2 %.

It should also be appreciated that the recession prone auto industry and many other US corporations are now in better financial shape and are less dependent on domestic sales than was the case in 1990. If speculative enthusiasm does not lift price/earnings ratios to a dangerous level, there is a possibility that the market's response to a near term recession might be more nearly a correction than an old fashioned crash.

4.8   CONCLUDING REMARKS

The relatively small stock market correction associated with the Fed's preemptive strike against the possibility of accelerating inflation in 1994 and the rather spectacular new high bubble of 1995 have tarnished the image of low dividend yields and a number of other market timing signals. While most investors are probably well advised to follow the philosophy of Peter Lynch and Jeremy Siegel, by investing in stocks for the long run, it can be interesting and possibly rewarding to have an appreciation of how the market has behaved over long periods of time.

The stock market bubbles identified by new high peaks that are separated by cumulative declines of three percent or more in Table 4.1 are one of the easiest data bases to update and maintain. They can be used to measure the duration, stability and magnitude of both short lived and more prolonged bull markets. They can also be used to obtain a quick, rough approximation of the gains and losses that "might have been obtained" in connection with a much wider range of statistical indicators, investment timing and trading strategies than can possibly be evaluated in this study.

Our attempt to differentiate between small and big bubbles and between minor corrections and major crashes would strongly suggest that beating the market is not an easy matter. We are inclined, however, to stick with the notion that the jury is still out as to whether changes in the S&P composite stock price index resemble a random walk and are truly consistent with the efficient market hypothesis. The nice thing about our tables is that they provide readers with enough history and cases to be in a better position to make an independent judgment with regard to a profound idea that has revolutionized courses in economics and finance but will no doubt remain controversial, forever and ever.

NOTE

1. An earlier version of this chapter was published jointly with Dr. Edward Renshaw in *The Journal of Investing*.

CHAPTER 5

Macroeconomic Determinants of Emerging Stock Markets: Theory and Evidence

5.1 INTRODUCTION

This chapter studies the relationship between stock market variables and macroeconomic activity in the "emerging markets" (developing markets). Financial as well as economic theory implies that macroeconomic variables like GNP, inflation, growth in money supply, changes in exchange rate should systematically affect the stock market returns. Changes or innovations being the cause of systematic risk in these variables should be suitably rewarded in the stock market. The studies done by Chen, Roll and Ross (1986), Chen (1991), Bailey and Chan (1993) show that in the case of developed countries especially U.S., U.K. and Japan, these sources of risk are significantly priced. Although the number of studies done on financial markets of developed countries is quite large, little attention has been paid so far to the emerging stock markets. This could be due to a lack of availability of data on emerging markets or because many of the developing markets were not open to foreign investors. However, in the past few years both of these limitations have been overcome.[1] This study analyses the performance of emerging stock markets with respect to their macroeconomic variables.

The primary goal of this chapter is to observe how the stock performance of emerging markets is being affected by the changing economic environment around them. Do emerging stock markets move with the macroeconomic variables of their respective countries or are they driven mostly by speculation and irrational behavior of their investors?[2] Do emerging stock markets reward their investors appropriately or not? How efficient and integrated are these markets? What is the correlation of returns with the global market returns? These are a few of the issues we would like to address here.

This study uses variables like risk, return and risk premium of the stock market as a means to measure the performance of the market. The list of macroeconomic variables include both monetary and real variables like inflation, growth in money supply, growth in GNP and the changes in exchange rate. We know that any systematic variable that affects the expected cash flows, dividends and discount factor will also have its indirect influence on the asset returns. Both real and monetary factors are expected to be related to the stock market variables.

The inflation rate and the growth in money supply should affect the nominal interest rate and also the expected cash flows by changing the value of the real assets of the company.[3] Growth in GNP will reduce the risk premium, improve the cash flows and also lower the discount factor. Finally the changes in exchange rate will influence dollar denominated returns. The appreciation or depreciation of the local currency which reflects the strength of the domestic economy is of great importance to foreign investors who get their return eventually in dollar terms.

This chapter is arranged in the following manner. Section II presents the data. Section III explains the methodology and the empirical results. Section IV talks about the efficiency of the emerging markets and their integration with the global markets. The final section gives a brief summary and conclusions.

5.2 DATA

This study is performed on the following 19 emerging stock markets: Argentina, Brazil, Chile, Colombia, Greece, India, Indonesia, Jordan, Korea, Malaysia, Mexico, Nigeria, Pakistan, Philippines, Portugal, Thailand, Turkey, Venezuela and Zimbabwe. The data on market returns and exchange rates for each country is obtained from IFC (International Finance Corporation), monthly EMDB (Emerging Market Data Base) files. Monthly data on risk free rate, industrial production, money supply M2, and the CPI is obtained from BESD (Bank Economic and Social Database) data set of the World Bank.

Industrial production is used as a proxy for GNP. Inflation is calculated by taking the first difference of the log of the CPI. The treasury bill rate is available only for Brazil, Greece, Mexico, Portugal, Thailand, Turkey and Zimbabwe. For the other countries we used money market rates or the deposit rate. For Jordan none of these series is available. Since industrial production and the money supply are both non stationary variables we use the growth rates for the money supply and industrial production which are difference stationary. Different countries have data available for different sample periods. Also, some of the macroeconomic variables are missing for a few countries. As we carry out the analysis we will elaborate on these points.

Global price indices like the Morgan Stanley Capital International (MSCI) index and the International Finance Corporation Global (IFCG) index are provided by IFC. Also, S&P 500 composite, FT 100 U.K. composite and Japan's Nikkei indexes are obtained from IFC. In order to get the monthly volatility of market returns, we used Schwert's (1989) procedure which is as follows: Estimate a 12th order autoregression for the returns including the dummy variables to allow for different monthly mean returns using all the data available for the series:

$$R_t = \sum_{j=1}^{12} \alpha_j D_{jt} + \sum_{i=1}^{12} \beta_i R_{t-i} + \varepsilon_t$$

where R_t is the monthly return on the market index in period t. D_{jt} is the dummy variable for the month j in period t, e.g.

$D_{1t} = 1$ for January
$D_{1t} = 0$ otherwise

The absolute value of the residuals $|\varepsilon_t|$ is the required estimate for the standard deviation for the month t.

5.3 METHODOLOGY AND EMPIRICAL RESULTS

According to financial and economic theory, the relationship between the stock market variables and the macroeconomic variables is not very clear. There are doubts even about the direction of the relationship.

The studies done by Body (1976), Nelson (1976), Fama and Schwert (1977), Fama (1981) and Fama (1990) on developed markets throw some light on this subject but there is a lot more to be said about emerging market behavior. For example we expect financial assets to be a hedge against inflation so that as inflation goes up, the return on assets will go up to prevent a fall in real returns. In the case of the U.S. economy this has not happened. The relation between inflation and real asset returns has in fact been negative in U.S. market. We would like to see if the emerging stock markets behave any different. Assuming that the money supply and inflation move together it will be interesting to examine the impact of the money supply on stock market variables. GNP growth is expected to have a positive influence on returns whereas the change in exchange rate, which is measured as the value of domestic currency per dollar, should be negatively correlated with returns measured in dollars. We also expect market risk and the risk premium to be positively related to growth in the money supply, inflation and changes in exchange rate.

5.3.1 Descriptive Statistics

Table 5.1 presents descriptive statistics for the market returns of all the emerging markets. Each return index is measured by IFC and includes dividends. Argentina has the highest monthly mean returns, 5.7%, undoubtedly it also has the highest volatility of 30% per month. It has a positively skewed distribution of returns and has the highest kurtosis. Mexico, which has comparable return of 4.8% per month, has half the standard deviation of the returns for Argentina. The Colombia and Chile indices have a return of 4% or more whereas their volatility stays around 8-10%. Overall, Latin American countries look more promising as compared to the other emerging markets from the investors point of view.

Among Asian countries, Philippines has the highest mean return and the second highest volatility after Taiwan. Zimbabwe's index performs better than Nigeria's index since it gives higher returns and has lower volatility. Greece has the highest returns and volatility among Middle East countries. The U.S. and U.K.'s performance is very close though U.K. performs a little better in terms of volatility. Japan shows low mean returns and higher volatility as compared to other developed countries and also the developed country global index i.e MSCI. The global index for developing countries, IFCG, shows greater mean returns and volatility in comparison to the global index for the developed countries, MSCI.

Table 5.1: Descriptive Statistic of Returns for the Period 1986.01-1992.12

Country	Mean	Std.dev	Skewness	Kurtosis
ARG	.057	.30	2.81	14.01
BRAZ	.022	.224	.39	0.13
CHIL	.04	.082	.004	-.08
COL	.042	.096	1.60	3.66
GRE	.029	.144	1.35	3.10
IND	.013	.102	.63	1.07
JOR	.003	.05	.20	1.67
KOR	.02	.09	.45	-.23
MAL	.014	.076	-.82	2.81
MEX	.048	.14	-1.15	5.78
NIG	.002	.11	-1.69	10.25
PAK	.02	.07	2.04	9.05
PHIL	.038	.11	.42	1.91
PORT	.028	.14	1.62	5.58
TAIW	.03	.16	.20	.77
THAI	.03	.09	-1.04	3.01
VENE	.032	.13	.75	1.74
ZIMB	.003	.075	-.54	.79
US	.01	.05	-1.05	4.54
UK	.01	.058	-1.08	4.39
JAP	.005	.07	-0.29	.91
MSCI	.01	.06	-.03	-0.12
IFCG	.012	.07	-0.63	1.34

5.3.2 Pooled Regressions

First of all we divided all the emerging markets into four groups based on their regions. The four categories are Asia, Africa, Latin America and Middle East. Asia includes India, Indonesia, Korea, Malaysia, Pakistan, Philippines and Thailand. Africa has only Nigeria and Zimbabwe. Latin America consists of Argentina, Brazil, Chile, Colombia, Mexico and Venezuela. Finally the Middle East has Greece, Jordan, Portugal and Turkey. The pooled regressions are done on balanced data which include monthly observations from January 1986 to December 1992 for Asia and Africa. The balanced data for Latin America is available from July 1987 to December 1992 and for the Middle East from January 1988 to December 1992. The following regressions were run on the pooled data of each region:

$$R_{it} = \alpha + \beta_1 (INF)_{it} + \beta_2 (\Delta \ln M_2)_{it} + \beta_3 (\Delta EX)_{it} + u_{it} \quad (5.1)$$

$$\sigma_{it} = a + b_1 (INF)_{it} + b_2 (\Delta \ln M_2)_{it} + b_3 (\Delta EX)_{it} + e_{it} \quad (5.2)$$

$$(R_{it} - Rf_{it}) = c + \gamma_1 (INF)_{it} + \gamma_2 (\Delta \ln M_2)_{it} + \gamma_3 (\Delta EX)_{it} + \eta_{it} \quad (5.3)$$

where i stands for different countries and t for time. R_{it} is the market return of country i at time t. σ_{it} represents the volatility, $(R_{it} - Rf_{it})$ is the risk premium, INF is inflation, M_2 is the money supply and EX is the exchange rate.

The results of equation (5.1) are presented in Table 5.2. Asian countries show that the asset returns are not significantly related to the macroeconomic variables. Africa results show that inflation has no impact on the asset returns. Growth in the money supply has a positive impact on returns and the change in exchange rate has negative effect on returns as expected.

For Latin American countries there is not enough information available on money supply in terms of balanced data so we could not estimate β_2. The results for inflation and the change in exchange rate show no significant effect on Latin American returns. Finally the Middle East countries, show that the asset returns are significantly negatively affected by the change in exchange rate. Inflation and money supply have no significant effect on Middle East countries' asset returns.

Table 5.2: Pooled Regression Results

$$R_{it} = \alpha + \beta_1 (INF)_{it} + \beta_2 (\Delta \ln M_2)_{it} + \beta_3 (\Delta EX)_{it} + u_{it}$$

Region	β_1	β_2	β_3	N	R^2
Asia	-.84	-.10	-.002	504	.01
86.01-92.12	(1.38)	(0.42)	(1.48)		
Africa	-.15	.31	-.07	168	.39
86.01-92.12	(0.71)	(2.03)	(9.78)		
Latin Am	.06	NA	0	396	.002
87.07-92.12	(.78)	& (.78)	&		
Mid East	.47	.01	-.005	180	.07
88.01-92.12	(0.81)	(0.19)	(3.55)		

The results of equation (5.2) are presented in Table 5.3. In Asia macroeconomic variables appear to have no significant effect on the volatility of the market. In the case of Africa, both Nigeria and Zimbabwe show that an increase in the exchange rate increases the volatility of their markets. This is consistent with financial theory. If the change in the exchange rate goes up, implying that the local currency is depreciating, investors will have a reason to believe that the local economy is not doing well. This will raise investment risk and the risk premium. However inflation and growth in the money supply do not affect volatility in the African markets. In Latin American and Middle East countries inflation has a significant positive effect on the volatility of the market.

The last market variable we looked at is the risk premium. Estimates for equation (5.3) are presented in Table 5.4. Asia's risk premium also shows no significant relationship with its macroeconomic variables. In the African countries the risk premium is positively correlated with growth in the money supply and negatively correlated with changes in the exchange rate. This is consistent with our hypothesis. In Latin America the risk premium is negatively related with inflation. In the Middle East changes in the exchange rate are

Studies on the Behavior of Equity Markets

Table 5.3: Pooled Regression Results

$$\sigma_{it} = a + b_1(INF)_{it} + b_2(\Delta \ln M_2)_{it} + b_3(\Delta EX)_{it} + e_{it}$$

Region	b_1	b_2	b_3	N	R^2
Asia	.21	-.05	.0003	504	.001
86.01-92.12	(0.60)	(0.41)	(0.35)		
Africa	-.06	.03	.04	168	.21
86.01-92.12	(0.42)	(0.24)	(6.67)		
Latin Am	.53	NA	-.0001	396	.21
87.07-92.12	(10.15)		(1.94)		
Mid East	.87	-.02	.001	180	.03
88.01-92.12	(2.21)	(0.60)	(0.67)		

Table 5.4: Pooled Regression Results

$$(R_t - Rf_{it}) = c + \gamma_1(INF)_{it} + \gamma_2(\Delta \ln M_2)_{it} + \gamma_3(\Delta EX)_{it} + \eta_{it}$$

Region	γ_1	γ_2	γ_3	N	R^2
Asia	-.96	-.16	-.002	504	.011
86.01-92.12	(1.65)	(0.72)	(1.54)		
Africa	-.12	.30	-.08	168	.40
86.01-92.12	(0.61)	(2.04)	(10.03)		
Latin Am	-.24	NA	0	396	.04
87.07-92.12	(3.95)		(1.08)		
Mid East	.13	.005	-.006	180	.08
88.01-92.12	(0.23)	(0.12)	(3.84)		

negatively related to the risk premium in a significant way. Inflation and money supply are not significantly related to the risk premium.

Our next step is to explore the relationships between the stock market variables and the economic variables for each individual country.

5.3.3 INDIVIDUAL COUNTRY RESULTS

The strength of the relation between a country's economic variables and its stock market variables reflects the extent to which markets are driven by rational factors. The following equations are estimated to explore this relationship:

$$R_t = \alpha + \beta_1 (INF)_t + \beta_2 (\Delta \ln M_2)_t + \beta_3 (\Delta EX)_t + \beta_4 (\Delta \ln IP)_t + u_t \ (5.4)$$

$$\sigma_t = a + b_1 (INF)_t + b_2 (\Delta \ln M_2)_t + b_3 (\Delta EX)_t + b_4 (\Delta \ln IP)_t + e_t \ (5.5)$$

$$(R_t - Rf_t) = c + \gamma_1 (INF)_t + \gamma_2 (\Delta \ln M_2)_t + \gamma_3 (\Delta EX)_t + \gamma_4 (\Delta \ln IP)_t + \eta_t$$
$$(5.6)$$

Table 5.5 presents the results for equation (5.4). Inflation has no significant relation with the emerging market retuns except in the case of Jordan where it is positively correlated with the returns. Jordan's financial assets have been hedge against inflation. Growth in the money supply is significantly positively correlated with asset returns in Argentina, Brazil, Chile and Venezuela. Since inflation and the money supply are expected to move together, the Latin American countries should have returns and inflation moving in the same direction. β_3 turns out to be significant in 11 out of the 19 countries showing a strong relation between changes in the exchange rate and the market returns for the respective countries.

Table 5.6 shows the results for equation (5.5). For Mexico there is a positive relation between risk and inflation. Malaysia's inflation is significantly negatively correlated with the market risk. The other countries show no relation between risk and inflation. Growth in the money supply is positively related to volatility in Argentina but has a significant negative relation in Greece. Other emerging markets show no relationship between risk and growth in the money supply. In

Table 5.5: Individual Country Regression Results

$$R_t = \alpha + \beta_1(INF)_t + \beta_2(\Delta \ln M_2)_t + \beta_3(\Delta EX)_t + \beta_4(\Delta \ln IP)_t + u_t$$

Country	β_1	β_2	β_3	β_4	N	R^2	DW-stat
ARG	-.34	1.05	-.83	NA	74	.08	2.21
	(0.95)	(2.04)	(1.36)				
BRAZ	-.42	1.26	2.00	.44	59	.18	2.03
	(0.81)	(3.35)	(.45)	(1.22)			
CHIL	-.72	.73	-.004	NA	168	.10	1.53
	(1.12)	(2.57)	(3.15)				
COL	-1.27	.31	-.01	NA	29	.33	2.07
	(1.56)	(1.19)	(2.93)				
GRE	-.61	.31	-.006	NA	202	.08	1.73
	(1.18)	(1.21)	(3.60)				
IND	-.28	.51	.01	.05	204	.02	1.82
	(0.45)	(1.33)	(1.15)	(.72)			
INDO	-1.64	NA	.0003	NA	35	.01	1.52
	(0.59)	(0.19)	(1.15)				
JOR	.57	.37	-1.78	-.01	168	.14	1.88
	(2.60)	(1.40)	(4.46)	(0.38)			

Table 5.5 (continued)

Country	β_1	β_2	β_3	β_4	N	R^2	DW-stat
KOR	-1.24 (1.62)	.21 (0.57)	-.001 (2.08)	NA	204	.04	2.09
MAL	2.32 (0.93)	.12 (0.22)	-.37 (1.40)	-.05 (0.46)	94	.04	1.9
MEX	.64 (1.40)	.09 (0.46)	-.65 (3.75)	-.05 (0.15)	123	.11	1.80
NIG	-.01 (0.05)	.34 (1.48)	-.07 (9.12)	NA	92	.51	1.85
PAK	-1.23 (1.49)	.01 (0.04)	-.01 (0.19)	NA	96	.02	1.53
PHIL	1.46 (0.75)	-.21 (0.43)	-.03 (1.42)	NA	72	.04	1.5
PORT	1.26 (0.30)	-.03 (0.44)	-.01 (1.60)	.14 (1.22)	54.07	.82	
THAI	NA	.20 (0.42)	-.03 (2.09)	NA	204	.02	1.76
TURK	-1.14 (0.89)	-1.10 (1.62)	.001 (1.87)	NA	63	.11	1.70
VEN	-.54 (1.09)	.97 (2.29)	-.03 (4.93)	NA	96	.24	1.62
ZIMB	-.32 (0.77)	.21 (0.91)	-.26 (3.26)	NA	118	.09	1.8

Table 5.6: Individual Country Regression Results

$$\sigma_t = a + b_1(INF)_t + b_2(\Delta \ln M_2)_t + b_3(\Delta EX)_t + b_4(\Delta \ln IP)_t + e_t$$

Country	b_1	b_2	b_3	b_4	N	R^2	DW-stat
ARG	.14	.79	-.72	NA	74	.27	1.9
	(0.60)	(2.44)	(1.85)				
BRAZ	.09	.33	.08	.21	59	.04	2.4
	(0.27)	(1.34)	(0.02)	(0.89)			
CHIL	.08	-.26	.0004	NA	168	.02	2.04
	(0.23)	(1.59)	(0.52)				
COL	-.95	.05	-.01	NA	25	.22	1.96
	(1.45)	(0.26)	(1.95)				
GRE	.45	-.42	.0002	NA	190	.03	1.95
	(1.24)	(2.36)	(0.21)				
IND	.42	-.11	.01	.08	192	.03	1.24
	(0.99)	(0.46)	(1.22)	(1.64)			
JOR	.26	.08	.34	.02	156	.04	1.7
	(1.84)	(0.48)	(1.36)	(0.85)			
KOR	.15	.08	.001	NA	192	.01	2.02
	(0.31)	(0.34)	(1.06)				
MAL	-4.64	-3.9	-.20	-.20	82	.25	1.9
	(3.72)	(1.51)	(1.46)	(3.79)			

Table 5.6 (continued)

Country	β_1	β_2	β_3	β_4	N	R^2	DW-stat
MEX	.97 (4.14)	-0.17 (1.61)	.46 (5.23)	.19 (1.02)	123	.31	2.08
NIG	-.18 (0.86)	-.01 (0.04)	.04 (5.52)	NA	80	.29	1.64
PAK	-.24 (0.49)	.29 (1.19)	.02 (0.88)	NA	84	.03	1.74
PHIL	1.54 (1.56)	-.35 (1.38)	00 (0.01)	NA	72	.06	2.30
PORT	-.83 (0.33)	-.04 (1.04)	-.0003 (0.12)	.09 (1.47)	42	.08	1.07
THAI	NA	-.22 (0.63)	.01 (0.63)	NA	192	.004	1.70
TURK	.12 (0.16)	.15 (0.37)	00 (0.58)	NA	51	.01	2.4
VEN	.30 (0.83)	-.39 (1.32)	-.01 (1.91)	NA	84	.07	1.63
ZIMB	-.17 (0.66)	.11 (0.72)	.05 (1.12)	NA	106	.02	2.03

Table 5.7: Individual Country Regression Results

$$(R_t - Rf_t) = c + \gamma_1 (INF)_t + \gamma_2 (\Delta \ln M_2)_t + \gamma_3 (\Delta EX)_t + \gamma_4 (\Delta \ln IP)_t + \eta_t$$

Country	$\gamma 1$	$\gamma 2$	$\gamma 3$	$\gamma 4$	N	R^2	DW-stat
BRAZ	-.43	.87	-5.10	.51	59	.17	2.10
	(0.86)	(2.37)	(1.19)	(1.45)			
CHIL	-1.12	.66	-.004	NA	168	.09	1.44
	(1.68)	(2.26)	(3.06)				
COL	-1.15	.34	-.01	NA	25	.31	2.05
	(1.17)	(1.21)	(2.74)				
GRE	-.35	.17	-.005	NA	89	.05	1.80
	(0.33)	(0.33)	(2.01)				
IND	-.33	.63	.01	.06	201	.02	1.75
	(0.52)	(1.55)	(1.13)	(.76)			
INDO	-1.67	NA	.0003	NA	35	.01	1.52
	(0.60)	(0.18)					
KOR	-1.45	.18	.001	NA	204	.05	2.10
	(1.90)	(0.49)	(2.10)				
MAL	2.32	.09	-.38	-.05	92	.04	1.9
	(0.92)	(0.17)	(1.40)	(0.45)			
MEX	-.13	.09	-.70	-.04	121	.13	1.90
	(0.29)	(0.47)	(4.11)	(0.10)			

Table 5.7 (continued)

Country	γ_1	γ_2	γ_3	γ_4	N	R^2	DW-stat
NIG	-.01 (0.06)	.32 (1.39)	-.08 (9.23)	NA	92	.51	1.87
PAK	-1.22 (1.48)	.03 (0.07)	-.01 (0.22)	NA	96	.02	1.53
PHIL	1.24 (0.64)	-.22 (0.44)	-.03 (1.45)	NA	72	.04	1.43
PORT	1.26 (0.30)	-.03 (0.44)	-.01 (1.60)	.14 (1.23)	54.07	.82	
THAI	NA	-.18 (0.34)	-.03 (2.30)	NA	153	.03	1.90
TURK	-1.15 (0.89)	-1.14 (1.67)	-.001 (2.06)	NA	63	.12	1.70
VEN	-.61 (1.23)	.89 (2.12)	-.03 (4.99)	NA	96	.24	1.63
ZIMB	-.38 (0.89)	.23 (0.97)	-.24 (3.03)	NA	117	.09	1.8

Table 5.8: Autocorrelations of the First Difference of the Market Price Index

Country	ρ_1	ρ_3	ρ_5	ρ_7	ρ_9	ρ_{11}
ARG	-.02	-.04	.01	.04	.11	-.02
BRAZ	.11	-.13	.05	.10	.06	-.04
CHIL	.25	-.01	-.04	.14	.006	-.06
COL	.36	-.14	.01	.24	-.04	-.06
GRE	.13	-.05	-.01	.03	.03	-.07
IND	.15	-.14	.07	.03	-.12	.05
JOR	.02	.19	-.08	-.08	-.06	-.01
KOR	-.07	-.01	.10	-.04	-.23	-.07
MAL	.06	-.11	.04	-.03	-.07	.07
MEX	.31	-.07	.06	-.04	.14	.01
NIG	.17	-.07	.09	-.02	.01	-.03
PAK	.20	-.30	.36	-.18	.01	-.02
PHIL	.30	.01	-.05	-.06	-.01	-.02
PORT	.17	-.27	.04	-.08	-.06	-.04
TAIW	.10	-.01	-.08	-.10	.09	.06
THAI	.18	-.12	-.19	.16	.15	.08
TURK	.21	.02	.06	.15	-.05	-.14
VENE	.17	.09	-.32	.02	.03	-.06
ZIMB	.15	.31	.11	.04	-.05	-.02

Table 5.9: Testing International CAPM Using IFCG as a Proxy for the World Index

$$(R_{it} - Rf_{it}) = \alpha_i + \beta_i[R_{wt} - Rf_{it}] + \varepsilon_{it}$$

Country	α	β	N	R^2	DW-stat	F-stat
BRAZ	-.03	.81	60	.36	2.03	33.52
	(0.87)	(5.79)				
CHIL	.02	.50	96	.18	1.60	21.44
	(3.03)	(4.63)				
GRE	.01	.09	91	.002	1.75	0.22
	(0.83)	(0.47)				
IND	.01	.12	93	.01	1.64	0.59
	(1.10)	(0.76)				
INDO	-.02	.38	35	.06	1.24	2.27
	(1.27)	(1.51)				
KOR	.01	.28	96	.05	2.07	4.84
	(1.18)	(2.20)				
MAL	.004	.49	92	.20	1.84	22.63
	(0.58)	(4.76)				
MEX	.02	.87	94	.21	1.51	25.31
	(1.88)	(5.03)				
NIG	-.01	-.15	96	.01	1.77	0.97
	(0.86)	(0.98)				

Table 5.9 (continued)

Country	α	β	N	R^2	DW-stat	F-stat
PAK	.01	-.02	96	.001	1.50	.06
	(1.78)	(0.25)				
PHIL	.02	.27	96	.03	1.36	2.74
	(2.27)	(1.65)				
PORT	.01	.76	82	.14	1.33	13.38
	(1.11)	(3.66)				
THAI	.02	.56	57	.24	1.87	17.52
	(1.78)	(4.18)				
TURK	.02	.86	66	.09	1.44	6.40
	(0.76)	(2.53)				
VEN	.01	-.33	96	.03	1.55	3.01
	(0.63)	(1.73)				

Table 5.10: Testing International CAPM Using MSCI as a Proxy for the World Index

$$(R_{it} - Rf_{it}) = \alpha_i + \beta_i[R_{wt} - Rf_{it}] + \varepsilon_{it}$$

Country	α	β	N	R^2	DW-stat	F-stat
BRAZ	-.07	.64	60	.25	1.97	19.94
	(1.78)	(4.47)				
CHIL	.02	.17	96	.01	1.45	1.48
	(2.43)	(1.22)				
GRE	.01	.29	91	.01	1.76	1.40
	(0.86)	(1.18)				
IND	.01	-.18	93	.01	1.67	1.07
	(1.18)	(1.03)				
INDO	-.03	.01	35	0	1.43	.001
	(1.79)	(0.04)				
KOR	.01	.45	96	.09	2.24	9.08
	(1.17)	(3.01)				
MAL	.004	.40	92	.09	1.75	8.91
	(0.54)	(2.98)				
MEX	.007	.27	94	.01	1.44	1.33
	(0.46)	(1.15)				
NIG	-.01	.18	96	.01	1.81	1.01
	(0.91)	(1.00)				

Table 5.10 (continued)

Country	α	β	N	R^2	DW-stat	F-stat
PAK	.01	.03	96	.001	1.50	.07
	(1.71)	(0.27)				
PHIL	.02	.58	96	.09	1.41	10.09
	(2.29)	(3.18)				
PORT	.02	.98	82	.17	1.44	16.87
	(1.29)	(4.11)				
THAI	.02	.23	57	.02	1.99	1.18
	(2.00)	(1.08)				
TURK	.01	.38	66	.01	1.50	.73
	(0.32)	(0.86)				
VEN	.01	-.16	96	.005	1.46	.50
	(0.68)	(0.70)				

Mexico and Nigeria, the change in the exchange rate is positively related with volatility as expected though there is no significant relationship in other emerging markets.

The data on industrial production was available for Brazil, India, Jordan, Malaysia, Mexico and Portugal. Only Malaysia shows significant negative relation between risk and growth in industrial production. This is consistent with the theory that an increase in the industrial production growth rate should reduce the market risk.

Finally Table 5.7 explains the results of equation (5.6). Inflation has no significant relationship with the risk premium except in the case of Korea where it has a marginally significant negative relationship. Growth in the money supply, as expected, is positively related with the risk premium in Brazil, Chile and Venezuela. Changes in the exchange rate are negatively related to the risk premium in nine emerging markets. Only in Korea, is the relationship positive. Growth in industrial production also has no significant effect on the risk premium. There is no risk free rate available for Argentina and Jordan so for these countries the estimation could not be done.

5.4 EFFICIENCY AND GLOBAL INTEGRATION

The analysis of the risk and return relationship for the emerging markets which are growing under completely different environment than the developed markets, could be very profitable for investors. The efficiency and the level of integration of these markets could enable investors to achieve higher returns for a given level of risk. Market efficiency implies that all relevant and ascertainable information is reflected in security prices and no one can make economic profits based on the readily available information. We performed a weak form efficiency test for the emerging markets stock price indices and tested whether

$$x_{i,t+1} = p_{i,t+1} - E\left[\tilde{p}_{i,t+1} \mid \Phi_t\right]$$

$$E\left[\tilde{x}_{i,t+1} \mid \Phi_t\right] = 0$$

where $x_{i,t+1}$ is the excess market value of the price index i at time $t+1$. It is the difference between the observed price and the expected value of the price that was projected at time t based on the information ϕ_t. The results show that all the markets are at least weak form efficient and follow a random walk. The autocorrelations of ΔP shown in Table 5.8 for all the emerging markets support the above results.

The issue that interests most foreign investors is how integrated the emerging markets are with the global or developed markets of the world. To find out the extent of their integration with both the developed and the developing countries, we tested the *International Capital Asset Pricing Model* using two different global indices as the market index. One is MSCI (Morgan Stanley Capital International) Index which contains only the developed countries of the world and the other is IFCG (International Finance Corporation Global) Index which contains only the developing countries of the world. According to ICAPM:

$$\left(R_{it} - Rf_{it}\right) = \alpha_i + \beta_i\left[R_{wt} - Rf_{it}\right] + \varepsilon_{it} \qquad (5.7)$$

where

$$\beta_i = \frac{cov\left(R_{wt}R_{it}\right)}{var\left(r_{wt}\right)}$$

Table 5.9 and Table 5.10 show the results for ICAPM. As expected the IFC global index is more correlated with the emerging markets since IFCG contains only the developing countries in its global index. MSCI which contains only the developed countries is not very significantly correlated with most of the emerging markets. Out of the 15 emerging markets analyzed here, only 5 are significantly positively related with MSCI; they are Brazil, Korea, Malaysia, Philippines and Portugal. Ten markets show a significant relationship with the IFC global index. Brazil, Chile, Indonesia, Malaysia, Mexico, Thailand, Turkey and Venezuela show much higher R^2 and correlations with IFCG than with MSCI. Only Venezuela shows negative and significant relationship with the IFCG world index.

Jensen's measure of performance α, which was expected to be zero turns out to be significantly different from zero for Chile, Mexico, Pakistan, Philippines and Thailand. This shows the above average performance of the markets in these countries and gives a *buy signal*.

Table 5.11: Correlation of Monthly Returns for the Period 1986.01-1992.12

NAME	ARG	BRA	CHI	COL	GRE	IND	JOR	KOR	MAL	MEX	NIG
ARG	1.00										
BRAZ	-.13	1.00									
CHI	-.02	.13	1.00								
COL	-.09	.10	.03	1.00							
GRE	.08	.02	.14	.23	1.00						
IND	.22	.05	.05	-.09	.04	1.00					
JOR	-.09	-.08	-.03	.06	.077	.001	1.00				
KOR	-.17	.01	.06	-.07	-.14	-.10	-.14	1.00			
MAL	-.04	.11	.22	.03	.04	.005	.07	.15	1.00		
MEX	.14	-.03	.31	.006	.13	.03	-.03	.19	.44	1.00	
NIG	.11	-.02	-.04	.13	.10	-.14	-.03	.07	-.16	-.10	1.00
PAK	.04	-.01	-.04	.38	-.08	-.06	.12	-.02	-.05	-.03	.001
PHI	-.10	.13	.22	.16	.14	-.06	.11	.17	.30	.07	.08
POR	-.01	.11	.21	.15	.42	-.08	-.05	.05	.21	.33	-.21
TAI	-.02	.06	.31	.11	.11	-.08	.13	.03	.24	.35	-.14
THA	.05	.07	.25	.11	.25	.08	.15	.05	.52	.35	-.14
VEN	.05	-.18	-.19	.11	.007	.03	-.07	-.11	-.12	-.09	.10
ZIM	-.08	-.11	-.06	-.09	.08	-.15	-.08	-.02	-.10	.02	.05
US	.06	.13	.27	.10	.15	-.11	.06	.25	.61	.41	.08
UK	.02	.07	.23	.006	.02	-.08	.13	.31	.63	.36	.03
JAP	-.11	.12	-.09	-.04	.07	-.16	.02	.36	.31	.22	.05
MSCI	-.11	.15	.06	.05	.14	-.15	.11	.29	.32	.16	.10
IFCG	.01	.38	.42	.08	.07	.04	.07	.25	.44	.47	-.11

Table 5.11 (continued)

NAME	PAK	PHIL	PORT	TAIW	THAI	VEN	ZIMB	US	UK	JAP	MSCI	IFCG
PAK	1.00											
PHI	.03	1.00										
POR	.03	.05	1.00									
TAIW	-.03	.07	.39	1.00								
THAI	.07	.25	.31	.41	1.00							
VEN	.003	-.14	-.03	-.20	-.20	1.00						
ZIM	-.07	.02	.15	.01	-.13	.24	1.00					
US	-.007	.28	.21	.11	.36	-.05	-.17	1.00				
UK	.02	.23	.26	.20	.44	-.11	-.15	.75	1.00			
JAP	-.19	.20	.22	.25	.22	-.11	.03	.24	.19	1.00		
MSCI	.02	.31	.42	.21	.29	-.09	.04	.44	.46	.56	1.00	
IFCG	-.02	.16	.38	.81	.45	-.27	-.17	.34	.41	.31	.26	1.00

Table 5.11 shows the correlation between the returns of the different countries and the world index returns for the period January 1986 to December 1992.

5.5 CONCLUSIONS

As is clear from the empirical results, not all of the emerging markets behave in the same manner. The Asian markets, in particular, respond very little to macroeconomic variables as compared to other emerging markets. None of the market returns are significantly related to inflation. Changes in the exchange rate and dollar measured returns show a significant negative relation in African and Middle Eastern countries. Growth in the money supply also has no impact on returns except in Africa.

Risk and inflation are positively related in Latin America and Middle East. There is barely any relation between risk and the growth in the money supply in emerging markets. In Africa, changes in the exchange rate respond positively to volatility in the market. Others show no significant impact on volatility.

The returns for African, Latin American and Middle Eastern countries appear to be more related with macroeconomic variables than in the case for Asian countries. In Asia, most of the markets have no significant relationship with the macroeconomic variables. Surprisingly, Africa performs rather well in terms of being significantly related to the macroeconomic variables.

All markets pass the weak form efficiency test. This implies that the emerging markets, even if driven by speculation and irrational behavior, at least follow the random walk. As far as integration is concerned, emerging markets are certainly more integrated with the developing countries' world index than with the developed countries' world index. The negative correlation between the emerging markets and different world indices shows the extent to which portfolios can be further diversified and made profitable.

NOTES

1. Fundamental structural changes like equity market liberalization in Korea, India, Mexico and Brazil have made it easy for the international investor to buy and sell in emerging markets.

2. According to John Mullin (1993), the cumulative returns in the emerging markets are correlated with their fundamentals. However, the

outstanding performances experienced by these countries surpass levels that can be explained by measures of ex-ante risk and ex-post macroeconomic performance.

3. Chen, Roll and Ross (1986) also argued that changes in price level will have a systematic effect which will change the asset valuation.

CHAPTER 6

Impact of Equity Market Liberalization: Case of Korea

6.1 INTRODUCTION

In recent years, the governments of Korea, Brazil, India, Pakistan, Argentina and Colombia have been trying to make the new market oriented economic plans more attractive by loosening restrictions on direct foreign investment in their equity markets.

Korea is the biggest emerging market and the world's twelveth biggest stock market. Due to its fast and recent emergence, Korea appears as an interesting country to researchers and academicians for the purpose of analyzing the impact of changing government policies on the equity market performance.[1] One main issue of concern among analysts these days is how the opening up of the equity market to foreign investors is affecting the host country's market performance.

There are a number of studies done on the Korean stock market. See e.g. Lee (1987), Lee (1989), Lee (1990a), Chung (1991), Christopher (1991) and more recently Ryser (1992), Sargent (1992), Jun (1992), Frankel (1993). After years of procrastination, the Korean equity market was eventually opened to the foreign investors in January 1992.[2] This permitted direct purchases of shares listed on the Korean stock exchange by foreign individuals. However, the purchases were subject to the following conditions:

1. No single investor can have more than 3% of the total outstanding shares of any listed company.

2. Aggregate foreign ownership is limited to 10% of the total outstanding shares of each class and each listed company. In certain cases the limit is only 8%. The lower limit is applied to companies which are considered important for public interest.

The two most important reasons for opening up the market were, first, the government of Korea was relying too heavily on outside loans as a source of foreign capital. The ratio of foreign investment in equity markets in Korea to the size of the economy was much smaller than for other new industrial countries. Secondly, the percentage of equity investment to the total outstanding debt was very small by international standards.

This chapter begins with a detailed analysis of the market data. We divided the Korean companies listed under IFC index into three categories: Small, medium and large, based on their capitalization of 1992. In order to see whether the risk-return relationship of the Korean companies is consistent with financial theories, the CAPM model was tested for each category for the periods before and after the liberalization. The *International Asset Pricing Model* was also tested to see if the Korean market has become more integrated with the global markets after the opening up. Contrary to our expectations, we find that the correlation of the Korean stock price index return with the global index return has gone down instead of going up. We also checked the correlation of KSPI with the developed countries' indices and found that the correlation has only increased with U.K. index. Japan and U.S. indices have become less correlated with KSPI after January 1992.

Apart from these, there are few other issues that have been explored in this study which will be explained as we carry out the analysis. This chapter is arranged in the following manner. Section II explains the data and various proxies. Section III examines the impact of market opening to foreign investors. Section IV gives a detailed analysis of the individual stocks. The final section reports the conclusions of this chapter.

6.2 DATA

The data for the price index, dividend yield, price earnings ratio, market capitalization, exchange rate, return on individual companies is all obtained from International Finance Corporation (IFC) emerging market data base (EMDB) monthly files. The short term money market rate obtained from international financial statistics is used as a proxy for the Korea's risk free rate. The money market rate is the rate at which the short term borrowings occur between financial institutions. Even though it is not completely risk free, it is the best proxy available for the risk free rate.

Data on foreign incoming and outgoing foreign investment is obtained from *Korea Securities Supervisory Board*. Global price indices like Morgan Stanley Capital International (MSCI) index and International Finance Corporation Global (IFCG) index are provided by IFC. Also, *S&P* 500 composite, FT 100 U.K. composite and Japan's Nikkei indexes are obtained from IFC. In order to get the monthly volatility for the Korean market return and IFC portfolio return, we used Schwert's (1989) procedure which is as follows. Estimate a 12th order autoregression for the returns including the dummy variables to allow for different monthly mean returns using all the data available for the series:

$$R_t = \sum_{j=1}^{12} \alpha_j D_{jt} + \sum_{i=1}^{12} \beta_i R_{t-i} + \varepsilon_t$$

where R_t is the monthly return on the market index in period t. D_{jt} is the dummy variable for the month j in period t, e.g.

$D_{1t} = 1$ for January
$D_{1t} = 0$ otherwise

The absolute value of the residuals $|\varepsilon_t|$ is the required estimate for the standard deviation for the month t.

P is the IFC stock price index for Korea measured in US dollars. It includes 134 stocks while Korean stock price index (KSPI) has 694 stocks. Return on KSPI has been used as a proxy for the market return since it contains a bigger sample of the market. Most of the variables are available from January 1986 to April 1993 except the data on the risk free return which is available only after November 1986.

6.3 IMPACT OF STOCK MARKET OPENING

6.3.1 Descriptive Statistic

Table 6.1 shows the amount of foreign incoming and outgoing investment for the period January 1992 to April 1993. Table 6.2 shows the descriptive statistics for the overall period while Table 6.3 and Table 6.4 show it for the period before and after the equity market was opened up to foreign investors. The mean return on the KSPI has gone up after liberalization. The expected volatility of return on KSPI also has gone up which is consistent with the *capital asset pricing model* (CAPM).

The return distribution of both IFC and KSPI has become a little more positively skewed after liberalization. The kurtosis of return on IFC index went up from 2.46 to 3.40 after liberalization. The optimal value of the kurtosis is 3, which means after liberalization, the tails of the return distribution became slightly thicker implying more frequent observations with small absolute returns and occasional large absolute returns. The mean and standard deviation of the price earnings ratio went down after opening while the expected dividend yield went up. The distribution of both price earnings ratios and dividend yields was positively skewed before liberalization but became negatively skewed after 1992. The kurtosis of the dividend yield before liberalization was close to 3.0 which is the ideal value for kurtosis but it changed to 4.32 after January 1992.

Table 6.6 and Table 6.7 show the autocorrelation using 12 lags of all the variables before and after the liberalization respectively. The autocorrelation functions of KSPI and IFC price index show that both follow a random walk before and after the liberalization. This shows that the Korean equity market is *weak form efficient*. For the period prior to January 1992 the price earnings ratio and dividend yield have autocorrelations dying out gradually. This makes one suspicious about the presence of an integrated component. The *Augmented Dickey Fuller* test done on both price earnings and dividend yield confirms a unit root for both the variables. Nevertheless, after January 1992 both the price earnings ratio and dividend yield became stationary implying that the mean and variance of these variables are not a function of time anymore.

Table 6.1: Foreign Investment in Korea after Equity Market Liberalization

Month	Incoming Investment U.S. $ million	Outgoing Investment U.S. $ million	Net Investment U.S. $ million
1992.1	425.1	35.7	389.4
1992.2	202.9	16.0	186.9
1992.3	128.9	24.2	104.7
1992.4	135.5	47.6	87.9
1992.5	89.4	34.2	55.2
1992.6	65.6	48.3	17.3
1992.7	70.1	67.9	2.2
1992.8	89.4	52.3	37.1
1992.9	124.3	40.7	83.6
1992.10	361.0	49.7	311.3
1992.11	582.0	139.9	442.1
1992.12	449.5	96.4	353.1
1993.1	465.2	146.5	318.7
1993.2	324.5	129.8	194.7
1993.3	647.0	157.4	489.6
1993.4	770.0	167.4	602.6

Table 6.2: Descriptive Statistic of Variables for the Period 1986.01-1993.04

RET   — Return on IFC index measured in U.S. dollars.
RETLC   — Return on IFC index measured in local currency won.
RETM   — Return on the Korean local market index.
SD   — Standard deviation of RET.
SDLC   — Standard deviation of RETLC.
SDM   — Standard deviation of RETM.
P/E   — Price earnings ratio of the stocks in the IFC index.
DIVYD   — Average dividend yield of the stocks in the IFC index.
P   — IFC price index measured in U.S. dollars.
PLC   — IFC price index measured in WON.
KSPI   — Korean stock price index.
R_f — Short term money market rate used as a proxy for risk free rate.

	Mean	Std.dev	Maximum	Minimum	Skewness	Kurtosis
RET	.017	.09	.265	-.19	.442	2.71
RETLC	.016	.088	.264	-.18	.495	2.85
RETM	.02	.083	.21	-.18	.33	2.50
SD	.07	.051	.256	.003	1.06	4.17
SDLC	.069	.051	.247	.003	.964	3.79
SDM	.055	.04	.168	.0003	.692	2.74
P/E	21.66	6.44	44.04	9.79	1.21	4.54
DIVYD	1.79	1.00	5.07	0.4	.486	3.18
P	410.84	148.49	703.63	124.95	.194	2.24
PLC	366.81	105.73	572.45	134.23	.005	2.29
KSPI	614.28	212.45	1003.31	160.42	-.394	2.48
R_f	.010	.002	.016	.007	.318	2.32

Table 6.3: Descriptive Statistic of Variables Before Market Opening 1986.01-1991.12

RET — Return on IFC index measured in U.S. dollars.

RETLC — Return on IFC index measured in local currency won.

RETM — Return on the Korean local market index.

SD — Standard deviation of RET.

SDLC — Standard deviation of RETLC.

SDM — Standard deviation of RETM.

P/E — Price earnings ratio of the stocks in the IFC index.

DIVYD — Average dividend yield of the stocks in the IFC index.

P — IFC price index measured in U.S. dollars.

PLC — IFC price index measured in WON.

KSPI — Korean stock price index.

R_f — Short term money market rate used as a proxy for risk free rate.

	Mean	Std.dev	Maximum	Minimum	Skewness	Kurtosis
RET	.019	.088	.213	-.19	.318	2.46
RETLC	.017	.087	.225	-.18	.388	2.61
RETM	.021	.084	.21	-.18	.289	2.52
SD	.067	.049	.215	.003	.856	3.09
SDLC	.066	.049	.204	.003	.788	2.79
SDM	.053	.036	.143	.0003	.89	3.35
P/E	22.13	6.97	44.04	9.79	.995	3.74
DIVYD	1.77	1.05	5.07	0.4	.621	3.03
P	419.14	161.82	703.63	124.95	.046	1.91
PLC	369.63	115.11	572.45	134.23	-.056	1.99
KSPI	613.46	233.42	1003.31	160.42	-.353	2.07
R_f	.010	.002	.016	.007	.318	2.32

Table 6.4: Descriptive Statistic of Variables After Market Opening 1992.01-1993.04

RET   — Return on IFC index measured in U.S. dollars.
RETLC — Return on IFC index measured in local currency won.
RETM   — Return on the Korean local market index.
SD   — Standard deviation of RET.
SDLC   — Standard deviation of RETLC.
SDM   — Standard deviation of RETM.
P/E   — Price earnings ratio of the stocks in the IFC index.
DIVYD — Average dividend yield of the stocks in the IFC index.
P   — IFC price index measured in U.S. dollars.
PLC   — IFC price index measured in WON.
KSPI   — Korean stock price index.
R_f — Short term money market rate used as a proxy for risk free rate.

	Mean	Std.dev	Maximum	Minimum	Skewness	Kurtosis
RET	.008	.100	.265	-.126	.881	3.40
RETLC	.011	.099	.264	-.124	.844	3.36
RETM	.013	.084	.198	-.099	.504	2.33
SD	.085	.058	.256	.01	1.36	5.29
SDLC	.083	.056	.247	.009	1.25	5.22
SDM	.063	.053	.168	.002	.413	1.82
P/E	19.55	2.26	23.62	15.25	-.20	2.22
DIVYD	1.92	.68	2.63	.07	-1.42	4.32
P	373.51	46.14	438.32	300.56	-.18	1.65
PLC	354.15	43.73	419.18	286.43	-.15	1.60
KSPI	617.96	62.26	721.6	509.95	-.27	1.98
R_f	.011	.001	.012	.009	-.65	1.84

Table 6.5: Autocorrelation of Variables for the Period 1986.01-1993.04

RET — Return on IFC index measured in U.S. dollars.
RETLC — Return on IFC index measured in local currency won.
RETM — Return on the Korean local market index.
SD — Standard deviation of RET.
SDLC — Standard deviation of RETLC.
SDM — Standard deviation of RETM.
P/E — Price earnings ratio of the stocks in the IFC index.
DIVYD — Average dividend yield of the stocks in the IFC index.

	$\rho 1$	$\rho 2$	$\rho 3$	$\rho 4$	$\rho 5$	$\rho 6$	$\rho 7$	$\rho 8$	$\rho 9$	$\rho 10$	$\rho 11$	$\rho 12$
RET	-.10	.14	-.08	.13	.04	.03	-.03	-.01	.16	.13	-.07	.05
RETLC	-.16	.11	-.11	.11	.03	.01	-.06	-.05	.14	.11	-.10	.04
RETM	-.10	.14	-.11	.14	.05	.07	.02	.01	.18	.20	-.001	.06
SD	.06	.05	-.01	-.07	.04	-.06	-.19	-.01	.03	.04	-.07	-.08
SDLC	.06	.05	.01	-.04	.02	-.08	-.21	-.01	.04	.03	-.05	-.09
SDM	-.07	-.17	.11	.04	-.01	.06	-.14	.09	.14	-.07	.03	-.03
P/E	.88	.79	.70	.61	.54	.48	.41	.34	.26	.15	.06	.01
DIVYD	.81	.73	.65	.56	.50	.45	.41	.37	.35	.30	.27	.25

Table 6.6: Autocorrelation of Variables Before Opening the Market 1986.01-1991.12

RET — Return on IFC index measured in U.S. dollars.
RETLC — Return on IFC index measured in local currency won.
RETM — Return on the Korean local market index.
SD — Standard deviation of RET.
SDLC — Standard deviation of RETLC.
SDM — Standard deviation of RETM.
P/E — Price earnings ratio of the stocks in the IFC index.
DIVYD — Average dividend yield of the stocks in the IFC index.

	$\rho 1$	$\rho 2$	$\rho 3$	$\rho 4$	$\rho 5$	$\rho 6$	$\rho 7$	$\rho 8$	$\rho 9$	$\rho 10$	$\rho 11$	$\rho 12$
RET	-.11	.13	-.09	.15	.04	.01	-.03	.06	.16	.21	-.09	.13
RETLC	-.18	.10	-.12	.13	.04	-.02	-.06	.03	.13	.20	-.13	.13
RETM	-.07	.13	-.12	.17	.07	.05	.01	.07	.17	.27	.01	.15
SD	.09	.01	-.05	.04	.05	-.09	-.28	-.13	.02	-.01	-.11	-.07
SDLC	.06	.02	-.04	.06	.05	-.12	-.28	-.13	.04	-.03	-.08	-.08
SDM	-.02	-.15	.01	.22	-.08	.02	-.02	-.07	.14	.05	-.07	-.12
P/E	.88	.79	.70	.61	.55	.49	.42	.35	.27	.16	.06	.01
DIVYD	.86	.77	.69	.60	.55	.49	.46	.42	.38	.34	.30	.29

Table 6.7: Autocorrelation of Variables After Opening Up the Market 1992.01-1993.04

RET — Return on IFC index measured in U.S. dollars.
RETLC — Return on IFC index measured in local currency won.
RETM — Return on the Korean local market index.
SD — Standard deviation of RET.
SDLC — Standard deviation of RETLC.
SDM — Standard deviation of RETM.
P/E — Price earnings ratio of the stocks in the IFC index.
DIVYD — Average dividend yield of the stocks in the IFC index.

	ρ_1	ρ_2	ρ_3	ρ_4	ρ_5	ρ_6	ρ_7	ρ_8	ρ_9	ρ_{10}	ρ_{11}	ρ_{12}
RET	-.04	.12	-.18	-.07	-.04	-.06	.04	-.24	.05	.03	.01	.01
RETLC	-.08	.12	-.19	-.06	-.02	-.05	.05	-.24	.04	.04	.01	.01
RETM	-.20	.15	-.12	-.11	-.04	-.13	.16	-.22	.07	.004	-.004	.03
SD	-.12	.02	.01	-.51	.01	-.17	.02	.22	.13	.02	.01	-.05
SDLC	-.06	-.02	.09	-.49	-.10	-.16	-.48	.23	.10	.03	.05	-.04
SDM	-.19	-.21	.19	-.34	.07	.10	-.30	.21	.05	-.25	.21	.05
P/E	.49	.24	.05	-.10	-.25	-.41	-.40	-.35	-.12	.02	.03	.05
DIVYD	.07	.10	-.04	-.07	-.13	-.21	-.21	-.13	00	-.02	.06	-.22

6.3.2 Changes in the Risk-Return Relationship

Table 6.8 shows the market price of risk for different periods. It increased from -0.62 to 0.17 after the opening up of the market. Though the bull period in Korean equity market started in mid 1980's, from 1987 to 1989 the boom in the market was noticeable. The KSPI composite broke through the 1000 level in April 1989 from its rebased level of 100 on January 4, 1980.[3] The average market price of risk for that period was 0.19, the highest so far. The negative market price of risk before the opening of the market is little puzzling. One reason could be that the proxy for the risk free rate i.e. the money market rate is not exactly risk free.

Table 6.9 presents the systematic risk on the IFC portfolio of Korean stocks. This is calculated using the CAPM model which is represented as:

$$R_p = Rf + \beta_p \left(R_m - R_f \right) + \varepsilon_t$$

where R_f is the risk free rate, R_p is the return on the IFC portfolio, R_m is the return on the KSPI, β_p is the systematic risk on the portfolio defined as $\beta_p = Cov(R_p, R_m)/Var(R_m)$ and e_t is the unsystematic risk on the portfolio.

Panel A of Table 6.9 shows the systematic risk of the IFC portfolio measured in U.S. dollars and Panel B presents the results for the IFC portfolio measured in the local currency won. The results of Panel A and B are not too different. Both of them show that the systematic risk has gone up significantly after the opening up of the market. Measured in U.S. dollars it increased from 0.94 to 1.14 whereas in local currency it increased from 0.91 to 1.13. To see if there is any structural shift in the systematic risk after 1992 we performed *Chow test*. The following hypothesis is tested:

$$H_0 : \beta_{Bl} = \beta_{Al}$$
$$H_A : \beta_{Bl} \neq \beta_{Al}$$

Table 6.8: Market Price of Risk

$$\lambda = \frac{E(R_m) - R_f}{\sigma_m}$$

R_m —   Return on the Korean local market index.
σ_μ —   Standard deviation of R_m.
R_f —   Short term money market rate used as a proxy for risk free rate.

Period	Mean	Maximum	Minimum
1987.01-1993.04	-0.45	51.05	-24.51
1987.01-1989.12	.19	5.33	-18.38
Before Opening	-0.62	5.33	-18.38
After Opening	.173	51.05	-24.51

Table 6.9: Systematic Risk (β)

$$R_{pt} = R_{ft} + \beta\left(R_{mt} - R_{ft}\right) + u_t$$

R_{pt} —	Return on the IFC portfolio.
R_{mt} —	Return on the Korean market index.
R_{ft} —	Risk free rate of return.
β —	Systematic risk on the IFC portfolio.
u_t —	Unsystematic risk on the IFC portfolio.

	Panel A: Currency U.S. dollars		
	Total Period 1986.11-1993.04	Before Opening 1986.11-1991.12	After Opening 1992.01-1993.04
β	.977	0.94	1.14
t-stat	(24.59)	(21.70)	(12.77)
R^2	.887	.885	.91
N	78	62	16
	Panel B: Local Currency Won		
β	.95	0.91	1.13
t-stat	(23.91)	(20.72)	(13.85)
R^2	.88	.875	.927
N	78	62	16

Table 6.10: Systematic Risk (β) of Large Companies

Name	Total Period 1986.11-1993.04	Before Opening 1986.11-1991.12	After Opening 1992.01-1992.12
POSCO	1.08	0.98	1.34
t-stat	(11.46)	(11.74)	(4.86)
Samsung Elec	0.83	0.87	0.64
t-stat	(9.11)	(8.76)	(2.80)
Hanil Bank	1.05	1.05	1.06
t-stat	(15.41)	(12.67)	(9.00)
Korea First	1.12	1.13	1.11
t-stat	(12.75)	(10.26)	(8.74)
Choheung Bank	1.05	1.06	1.00
t-stat	(14.11)	(12.39)	(6.49)
Commercial B	1.07	1.10	0.98
t-stat	(14.28)	(12.91)	(6.09)
Bank of Seou	1.03	1.06	0.95
t-stat	(13.22)	(11.78)	(5.89)
Kia Ind.	0.88	0.84	1.09
t-stat	(7.10)	(5.99)	(4.13)
Ssangyong Oi	0.70	0.68	0.76
t-stat	(5.68)	(4.59)	(3.32)
Lucky Ltd.	0.90	0.85	1.13
t-stat	(9.14)	(7.83)	(4.90)
Hyundai Moto	0.87	0.83	1.05
t-stat	(8.35)	(7.87)	(3.09)
Daewoo Secur	1.37	1.43	1.23
t-stat	(9.77)	(8.08)	(6.23)
KLTCB	0.94	1.00	0.76
t-stat	(9.34)	(8.73)	(3.66)
KAL	0.96	0.93	1.11
t-stat	(11.23)	(11.05)	(3.70)
Gold Star	0.93	0.92	0.98
t-stat	(7.78)	(7.33)	(2.72)
Daewoo Elect	0.98	1.01	0.86
t-stat	(8.19)	(7.85)	(2.57)
Lucky Secur	1.36	1.44	1.16
t-stat	(8.72)	(7.23)	(6.13)

Table 6.10 (continued)

Name	Total Period 1986.11-1993.04	Before Opening 1986.11-1991.12	After Opening 1992.01-1992.12
Daewoo Heavy	0.84	0.83	0.87
t-stat	(5.39)	(4.89)	(2.17)
Dongsuh Secur	1.34	1.41	1.18
t-stat	(13.54)	(12.50)	(5.60)
Ssangyong Cem	1.01	1.00	1.05
t-stat	(9.4)	(8.70)	(3.47)

where β_{Bl} stands for the systematic risk before liberalization and β_{Al} stands for the systematic risk after liberalization of the market. The Chow statistic used here is given as:

$$F = \frac{(SSE_R - SSE_1 - SSE_2)/K}{(SSE_1 - SSE_2)/(n + m - 2K)} \sim F_{k, n+m-2K}$$

SSE_R	=	The restricted sum of squared residuals.
SSE_1	=	Sum of squared residuals for the period before liberalization.
SSE_2	=	Sum of squared residuals for the period after liberalization.
K	=	Number of coefficients.
n	=	Number of observations belonging to period before liberalization.
m	=	Number of observations in the period after liberalization.

For the portfolio measured in U.S. currency, the F- statistic turned out to be 3.87 whereas the critical value of F at 95% confidence is 3.97. Since $F < F_c$, the null hypothesis of no structural change was accepted marginally. The same test when performed on the portfolio measured in won gave a different result. This time the F- statistic was 5.20. Now $F > F_c$ so we accepted the alternative hypothesis. This implies that the systematic risk did change after liberalization.

We also looked at the top 20 companies (based on their 1992 market capitalization) to see if their systematic risk increased after liberalization. Table 6.10 shows the results of these companies. It appears that for 50% of the companies the systematic risk increased and for the other 50% it decreased significantly.

6.3.3 Unsystematic Risk

The unsystematic risk on the IFC portfolio is presented in Table 6.11. The expected value of the unsystematic risk appears to be close to zero for both the periods. In order to confirm whether it is indeed zero or not, we carried out the t-test which is as follows:

$$t = \frac{\sqrt{n}(x - \mu_0)}{\sqrt{Var}}$$

Table 6.11: Unsystematic Risk

$$R_{pt} = R_{ft} + \beta\left(R_{mt} - R_{ft}\right) + u_t$$

R_{pt} — Return on the IFC portfolio.
R_{mt} — Return on the Korean market index.
R_{ft} — Risk free rate of return.
β — Systematic risk on the IFC portfolio.
u_t — Unsystematic risk on the IFC portfolio.

	Panel A: Currency U.S. dollars		
	Total Period 1986.11-1993.04	Before Opening 1986.11-1991.12	After Opening 1992.01-1993.04
Mean	-.004	-.003	-.005
Std.dev	.029	.028	.027
N	78	62	16
	Panel B: Local Currency Won		
Mean	-.005	-.006	-.002
Std.dev	.029	.028	.025
N	78	62	16

The hypothesis is:

$$H_0 : \mu_0 = 0$$
$$H_A : \mu_0 \neq 0$$

Accept H_0 if $-t_c \leq t \leq t_c$

The t-statistic confirms that the unsystematic risk is not significantly different from zero both before and after the liberalization and also for both kinds of currencies.[4] This result tells us that the Korean equity market was efficient both before and after the liberalization. The opening up of the market had practically no impact on the unsystematic risk, its mean value stayed close to zero even after January 1992.

6.3.4 Test for Granger Causality

In order to observe the impact of foreign incoming investment on market return and volatility we performed Granger Causality test. A variable 'x' Granger causes variable 'y' if variable 'x' helps in predicting variable 'y'. In other words,

$$y_t = a_1 y_{t-1} + a_2 y_{t-2} + \cdots + b_1 x_{t-1} + b_2 x_{t-2} + \cdots + e_t$$

'x' causes 'y' if $b_i \neq 0$ for some i.

The data includes observations from January 1992 to April 1993. The following regressions were estimated:

$$R_{mt} = a_1 R_{mt-1} + b_1 FII_{t-1} + u_{1t}$$
$$\sigma_{mt} = a_1 \sigma_{mt-1} + b_1 FII_{t-1} + u_{2t}$$

where R_{mt} is the return on the KSPI, FII is the foreign incoming investment and σ_{mt} is the volatility in the market. The results presented in Table 6.12 Panel A, show that foreign incoming investment does not have any impact on the future market returns. However, it does cause higher volatility in the market. A one billion dollar increase in foreign incoming investment causes the monthly volatility in return to go up by

Table 6.12: Granger Causality Results

Panel A: $Y_t = a_1 Y_{t-1} + b_1 FII_{t-1} + u_t$				
Y	a_1	b_1	R^2	F-stat
RETM	-0.28	.051	.08	.59
	(1.02)	(0.76)		
STDM	0.28	.13	.47	4.64
	(0.99)	(2.10)		
Panel B: $FIO_t = a_1 FIO_{t-1} + b_1 X_{t-1} + u_t$				
X	a_1	b_1	R^2	F-stat
RETM	1.03	.082	.61	.58
	(10.05)	(0.76)		
STDM	1.02	0.06	.60	.13
	(7.70)	(0.37)		
Panel C: $Y_t = a_1 Y_{t-1} + b_1 NI_{t-1} + u_t$				
Y	a_1	b_1	R^2	F-stat
RETM	-0.29	0.06	.08	.59
	(1.03)	(0.74)		
STDM	0.33	.15	.52	4.03
	(1.17)	(1.96)		

13%. Panel B of Table 6.12 explores the impact of the market return and the volatility on the foreign outgoing investment. The coefficients are clearly insignificant so we conclude that changes in market return and volatility do not cause any impact on the foreign outgoing investment.

Finally Panel C shows the results of any possible impact of net foreign investment on market return and volatility. Again it turns out that net foreign investment does not affect the future behavior of financial returns but does have a significant effect on the volatility. If the net foreign investment goes up by 1 billion dollars, the volatility in the market will go up by 15%.

6.3.5 Integration with Global Markets

One of the goals of the government of Korea was to make the Korean equity market more efficient and integrated. It was hoped that the market liberalization of 1992 would not only provide the much needed

Table 6.13: Correlation of Korean Stock Price Index with Global Markets

KSPI	— Korean stock price index.
IFCG	— International financial corporation global composite index.
MSCI	— Morgan Stanley capital international index.
S&P	— *S&P* 500 composite U.S. index.
UK	— *FT* 100 U.K. composite index.
JAPAN	— Japan's Nikkei index.

	Total Period 1984.12-1993.03	Before Opening 1984.12-1991.12	After Opening 1992.01-1993.03
KSPI, IFCG	.837	.880	.306
KSPI, MSCI	.896	.904	.072
KSPI, *S&P*	.456	.604	.474
KSPI, UK	.494	.599	.703
KSPI, JAPAN	.841	.935	.346

$$E(R_{kt}) = R_{ft} + \beta \left[E(R_{wt}) - R_{ft} \right]$$

	Total Period 1986.11-1993.03	Before Opening 1986.11-1991.12	After Opening 1992.01-1993.03
KSPI, IFCG	0.29	0.23	1.09
t-stat	(2.26)	(1.73)	(2.56)
R^2	.05	.04	.29
KSPI, MSCI	0.44	0.49	0.08
t-stat	(2.84)	(2.98)	(0.18)
R^2	.09	.12	.001

foreign capital to the market but also make the existing investors think more rationally. The importance of fundamentals in the market would rise while the speculation would go down. The correlation of the Korean market index with the world indices was also expected to go up after the liberalization.

Table 6.13 presents the results of the correlation between KSPI and various other global and developed countries' indices. It was surprising to note that the correlation between KSPI and other indices went down dramatically after liberalization. The only exception was the U.K. composite index. The correlation between KSPI and FT 100 increased from 0.59 to 0.70 after liberalization. The trend shows that British investors have always had the highest share among foreign investors in the Korean equity markets. It appears that after January 1992, the two markets started moving even closer to one another. KSPI and MSCI moved very close during late 1988 and early 1989 when the Korean market was booming but started growing apart again. Table 6.13 also shows the results of the *international capital asset pricing model* (ICAPM) which is represented as:

$$E(R_{kt}) = R_f + \beta\left(E(R_{wt}) - R_{ft}\right)$$

where $\beta = Cov(R_{kt}, R_{wt})/Var(R_{wt})$ and R_{wt} is the return on the world index.

The results show that β went up from 0.23 to 1.09 after liberalization when the return on IFCG was used as a proxy for R_{wt}. The R^2 also went up. Nevertheless, when MSCI was used as a proxy for R_{wt}, β turned out to be insignificant and R^2 went down.[5] A possible explanation is that the IFCG index contains only the developing markets whereas MSCI has only the developed country markets. Korea being one of the emerging markets, should be more integrated with IFCG than with MSCI.

6.4 ANALYSIS OF INDIVIDUAL STOCKS

The behavior of individual stocks has always attracted the attention of analysts, economists and academicians. The market index gives a good overall picture of the market but does not throw any light on the performance of the individual stocks. In this section we carry out a

Table 6.14: Twenty Largest Korean Companies Listed in IFC Index

$$R_{it} = \alpha + \beta_k R_{kt} + \beta_w R_{wt} + e_t$$

Name	N	Before Opening		After Opening	
		β_k	β_w	β_k	β_w
POSCO	41	0.98	-0.10	1.33	-1.26
t-stat		(11.43)	(0.85)	(6.04)	(2.66)
Samsung Elec	72	0.95	0.19	0.64	-0.13
t-stat		(8.23)	(1.15)	(2.69)	(0.26)
Hanil Bank	44	1.04	0.15	1.04	-0.25
t-stat		(12.42)	(1.29)	(8.85)	(0.98)
Korea First	44	1.13	0.10	1.10	-0.14
t-stat		(10.00)	(0.64)	(8.37)	(0.51)
Choheung Bank	44	1.05	0.21	0.98	-0.17
t-stat		(12.31)	(1.83)	(6.15)	(0.48)
Commercial B	44	1.09	0.22	0.96	-0.23
t-stat		(12.91)	(1.92)	(5.82)	(0.66)
Bank of Seou	44	1.05	0.25	0.93	-0.18
t-stat		(11.76)	(2.04)	(5.60)	(0.49)
Kia Ind.	72	0.90	0.17	1.04	-0.55
t-stat		(7.17)	(0.95)	(3.95)	(0.96)
Ssangyong Oi	41	0.71	-0.17	0.77	0.64
t-stat		(4.63)	(0.82)	(3.51)	(1.35)
Lucky Ltd.	72	0.93	0.35	1.10	-0.45
t-stat		(9.59)	(2.49)	(4.73)	(0.90)
Hyundai Moto	72	0.90	-0.03	1.01	-0.91
t-stat		(8.91)	(0.19)	(3.07)	(1.28)
Daewoo Secur	41	1.44	0.09	1.23	-0.16
t-stat		(7.86)	(0.35)	(6.05)	(0.36)
KLTCB	44	1.02	0.04	0.75	0.06
t-stat		(8.61)	(0.27)	(3.49)	(0.13)
KAL	72	1.08	0.30	1.08	-0.20
t-stat		(8.68)	(1.66)	(3.47)	(0.30)

Table 6.14 (continued)

Name	N	Before Opening		After Opening	
		β_k	β_w	β_k	β_w
Gold Star	72	0.97	-0.28	0.94	-0.36
t-stat		(7.62)	(1.52)	(2.53)	(0.45)
Daewoo Elect	72	1.16	0.23	0.82	-0.24
t-stat		(6.93)	(0.97)	(2.38)	(0.32)
Lucky Secur	41	1.48	0.08	1.17	-.001
t-stat		(7.20)	(0.27)	(5.93)	(0.002)
Daewoo Heavy	72	1.07	0.38	0.81	-0.87
t-stat		(5.72)	(1.40)	(2.03)	(1.01)
Dongsuh Secur	41	1.45	-0.08	1.19	0.16
t-stat		(12.53)	(0.53)	(5.44)	(0.35)
Ssangyong Cem	72	1.02	0.09	1.07	0.72
t-stat		(9.71)	(0.59)	(3.58)	(1.12)

Table 6.15: 17 Medium Size Korean Companies Listed in IFC Index

$$R_{it} = \alpha + \beta_k R_{kt} + \beta_w R_{wt} + e_t$$

Name	N	Before Opening		After Opening	
		β_k	β_w	β_k	β_w
Kolon Ind	44	0.97	-0.02	0.49	1.65
t-stat		(6.03)	(0.10)	(1.62)	(2.51)
Chungbuk Ban	41	1.11	0.19	1.01	0.17
t-stat		(10.79)	(1.39)	(6.61)	(0.51)
KDLC	24	1.28	0.27	0.82	0.86
t-stat		(8.55)	(1.34)	(4.03)	(1.94)
Daewoo Telec	13	0.87	-0.33	0.51	-0.39
t-stat		(3.32)	(0.85)	(1.13)	(0.40)
Orion Electr	13	0.72	0.05	0.60	0.79
t-stat		(2.70)	(0.13)	(2.15)	(1.30)
Taihan Elect	72	0.68	-0.16	0.91	-0.69
t-stat		(4.20)	(0.70)	(3.07)	(1.07)
Samsung Cons	41	0.89	-0.08	0.99	-0.48
t-stat		(8.24)	(0.56)	(3.19)	(0.72)
Gyeong Nam	13	1.05	0.33	0.93	-0.12
t-stat		(6.70)	(1.44)	(6.08)	(0.37)
Daelim Ind	44	1.01	0.20	1.17	-0.24
t-stat		(6.64)	(0.97)	(4.39)	(0.42)
Sun Kyung	72	1.13	-0.28	0.32	-0.09
t-stat		(10.02)	(1.74)	(0.78)	(0.10)
Dongkuk Stee	41	0.69	-0.13	1.33	0.07
t-stat		(5.70)	(0.77)	(2.91)	(0.07)
Dong A Const	41	1.07	0.08	1.39	-0.36
t-stat		(8.55)	(0.48)	(6.41)	(0.77)
Kwang Ju Ban	13	0.92	0.27	0.90	0.37
t-stat		(5.87)	(1.17)	(4.78)	(0.89)
Hana Bank	44	1.07	0.17	0.95	0.28
t-stat		(5.89)	(0.69)	(3.29)	(0.46)
Inchon Iron	41	0.60	0.05	0.56	-0.85
t-stat		(5.28)	(0.32)	(1.30)	(0.91)
Korea Pacifi	72	-1.71	-2.83	1.20	-0.05
t-stat		(0.99)	(1.13)	(3.47)	(0.06)
Hanshin Secur	13	1.60	0.03	1.25	-0.14
t-stat		(9.38)	(0.13)	(7.08)	(0.38)

Table 6.16: Twenty Smallest Korean Companies Listed in IFC Index

$$R_{it} = \alpha + \beta_k R_{kt} + \beta_w R_{wt} + e_t$$

Name	N	Before Opening		After Opening	
		β_k	β_w	β_k	β_w
Byuck San	72	0.92	-0.25	0.71	0.06
t-stat		(3.00)	(0.57)	(2.23)	(0.08)
Hanil Synthe	13	1.04	0.30	1.43	0.29
t-stat		(3.33)	(0.65)	(2.79)	(0.27)
Han Yang	72	1.49	-0.24	1.17	0.82
t-stat		(6.00)	(0.67)	(1.60)	(0.51)
Kwang Ju Hig	13	0.57	-0.03	1.39	0.73
t-stat		(1.38)	(0.05)	(2.72)	(0.66)
Hyosung Corp	41	0.75	-0.25	1.25	0.78
t-stat		(4.85)	(1.21)	(3.36)	(0.96)
Korea Steel	41	0.93	0.18	0.87	-0.35
t-stat		(6.91)	(0.97)	(1.97)	(0.36)
Sam Mi Corp	41	1.01	0.03	1.06	-0.09
t-stat		(5.66)	(0.12)	(2.39)	(0.09)
Hyundai Corp	72	0.95	-0.40	0.68	-0.24
t-stat		(9.81)	(2.89)	(2.68)	(0.44)
Lucky Metal	44	0.81	0.02	0.83	0.09
t-stat		(5.53)	(0.09)	(1.80)	(0.09)
Hanil Synthe	13	1.04	0.20	1.38	0.19
t-stat		(3.22)	(0.41)	(2.76)	(0.17)
Korea Machin	72	0.57	0.03	0.86	-0.86
t-stat		(4.42)	(0.15)	(2.21)	(1.01)
Han Shin Con	72	1.28	-0.06	1.06	1.06
t-stat		(6.98)	(0.22)	(1.44)	(0.67)
Dong Bu Stee	44	0.78	0.02	0.97	-0.39
t-stat		(5.82)	(0.11)	(3.59)	(0.67)
Ssang Young	13	1.42	-0.27	1.29	0.20
t-stat		(6.06)	(0.78)	(5.57)	(0.39)

Table 6.16: Twenty Smallest Korean Companies Listed in IFC Index

Name	N	Before Opening		After Opening	
		β_k	β_w	β_k	β_w
Hanil Develo	41	0.83	-0.05	1.12	0.01
t-stat		(5.81)	(0.25)	(1.83)	(0.01)
Hanshin Secu	13	1.61	0.15	1.19	0.10
t-stat		(7.28)	(0.46)	(6.28)	(0.24)
Saeil Heavy	44	0.92	0.25	1.25	0.60
t-stat		(5.66)	(1.12)	(2.67)	(0.59)
Cheil Synthe	44	0.80	-0.12	0.50	2.03
t-stat		(3.89)	(0.43)	(1.56)	(2.87)
Kwang Ju Hig	13	0.85	-0.06	1.51	0.93
t-stat		(2.02)	(0.11)	(2.98)	(0.85)
Poongsan Met	41	1.23	0.19	0.92	0.37
t-stat		(7.38)	(0.83)	(3.05)	(0.57)

Table 6.17: The liberalization of the Emerging Markets

Country	Opening Date	Magnitude of Opening
Argentina	Oct 1991	Fully opened.
Brazil	May 1991	100% of the non voting preferred stock, 49% of the voting common stock.
Chile	Dec 1988	25% of the listed companies' shares.
Colombia	Feb 1991	Fully opened.
Greece	Dec 1988	Fully opened.
India	Nov 1992	24% of the issued share capital.
Indonesia	Sept 1989	49% of all companies' listed shares.
Jordan	Dec 1988	49% investable.
Korea	Jan 1992	10% of the capital of listed companies, from July 1992, limit can go up to 25%.
Malaysia	Dec 1988	30% for banks and institutions, 100% for the other stocks.
Mexico	May 1989	30% for banks, 100% for the other stocks.
Nigeria	Closed	Closed for foreign investors.
Pakistan	Feb 1991	Fully opened.
Phillipines	Oct 1989	Investable upto 40%.
Portugal	Dec 1988	Fully opened.
Taiwan	Jan 1991	Investable upto 10%.
Thailand	Dec 1988	Investable upto 49%.
Turkey	Aug 1989	Fully opened.
Venezuela	Jan 1990	100% investable except bank stocks.
Zimbabwe	Closed	Closed to foreign investors.

detailed study of various individual stocks. First of all we look at the twenty largest Korean stocks listed in the IFC index. These stocks are likely to be heavily demanded by foreign investors. We estimate the following regressions:

$$R_{wt} = \delta + \gamma R_{kt} + \eta_t$$
$$R_{it} = \alpha + \beta_k R_{kt} + \beta_w UR_{wt} + \varepsilon_t$$

where R_{wt} is the return on MSCI index, R_{kt} is the return on the KSPI, R_{it} is the return on stock i and UR_{wt} represents the residuals from regressing the world market return on the Korean market return. UR_{wt} which is same as η_t represents that part of the world return which is not explained by the return in the Korean market. R_{kt} and UR_{wt} are orthogonal to one another. One would expect that after liberalization, the Korean betas of the large firms would go down while the world betas would go up. The reason being that after liberalization, the share of foreign investors in these stocks will increase which will increase the covariance between the individual stocks and the world index. At the same time, the share of domestic investors is falling which will decrease the covariance between the individual stocks and the Korean price index.

Table 6.14 presents the results for the top 20 companies in Korea. Out of those 20 stocks, 13 have β_k going down significantly after the liberalization while 15 have β_w going up but insignificantly. In order to check if the results are sensitive to the size of the stocks we also looked at the medium and small sized companies. Table 5.15 which displays the results of 17 medium sized companies shows that 12 stocks are going down in β_k and 12 are going up in β_w. Table 6.16 shows that out of 20 smallest companies 8 are going down in β_k and 13 are going up in β_w. The level of significance does not change much as the size of the companies change. The above pattern shows that a higher percentage of the large stocks behave as expected by the theory.

6.5 CONCLUSIONS

The government of Korea has taken progressive measures to internationalize the equity market of Korea. The recent opening of the equity market to foreign direct investment was the final step by the government towards liberalization.

The study done in this chapter points out several important findings. The foreign incoming investment since January 1992, has increased the volatility of the market without having any significant affect on the market return. The CAPM results show that the systematic risk of the market has gone up marginally after liberalization. The correlation of KSPI increased with the U.K. price index and decreased with the U.S. and Japan price indices. Also, there was a marginal increase in the value of KSPI.

Even though the small sample period after the liberalization was a major hinderance in this study, it gives us some insight into the Korean equity market. Looking at the rising value of the KSPI after January 1992 one can forecast that the KSPI will rise further in the future due to increased foreign demand.

NOTES

1. The low correlation between emerging markets and established equity markets will further diversify a global portfolio and help in reducing risk.

2. Table 6.17 shows the liberalization dates of some other emerging markets.

3. See Park and Agtmael (1993), chapter 5.

4. The test results are not presented here but are available with the author.

5. Park and Agtmael (1993), pointed out that the correlation of MSCI with IFC composite index which contains twenty emerging markets is only 0.27. They also said that there are economic reasons to believe that correlation coefficients do not necessarily increase as the emerging markets become a better known part of the global investment orbit.

Bibliography

[1]   Arrow, K.J. "The theory of risk aversion," *Individual Choice under certainity and uncertainity*, collected papers of K.J. Arrow, Cambridge, MA: Harvard University Press, 1984, 147-171.

[2]   Balvers, R.J., T.F. Cosimano and B. McDonald. "Predicting stock returns in an efficient market," *Journal of Finance*, (45), 1990, 1109-1128.

[3]   Bekaert, Geert and Robert J. Hodrick. "Characterizing predictable components in excess returns on equity and foreign exchange markets," *Journal of Finance*, (47), 1992, 467-510.

[4]   Beveridge, S. and C.R. Nelson. "A new approach to decomposition of economic time series," *Journal of Monetary Economics*, (7), 1981, 151-174.

[5]   Blanchard, O. "The traditional interpretation of macroeconomic fluctuations," *American Economic Review*, (79), 1989, 1146-1164.

[6]   Blanchard, O.J. and S. Fischer. *Lectures on Macroeconomics*, MIT press, 1989.

[7]   Blanchard, O. and D. Quah. "The dynamic effects of aggregate demand and supply disturbances," *American Economic Review*, (79), 1989, 665-673.

[8]   Body, Z. "Common stocks as a hedge against inflation," *Journal of Finance*, (31), 1976, 459-470.

[9]   Breeden, D.T. "An intertemporal asset pricing model with stochastic consumption and investment opportunities," *Journal of Financial Economics*, (7), 1979, 265-296.

[10]   Buckberg, Elaine. "Emerging stock markets and international asset pricing," *MIT, Unpublished manuscript*, 1992.

[11]   Campbell, J.Y. "Stock returns and term structure," *Journal of Financial Economics*, (18), 1987, 373-399.

[12]   Campbell, John Y. and Yasushi Hamao. "Predictable stock returns in the United States and Japan: A study of long term capital market integration," *Journal of Finance*, (47), 1992, 43-70.

[13]   Campbell, J.Y. and N.G. Mankiw. "Are output fluctuations transitory?," *Quarterly Journal of Economics*, (102), 1987, 857-880.

[14]   Campbell J.Y. and R.J. Shiller "Cointegration and tests of present value models," *Journal of Political Economy*, (95), 1987, 1062-1087.

[15]   Campbell, J.Y. and R. Shiller. "The dividend price ratio and expectations of future dividends and discount factors," *Review of Financial Studies*, (1), 1988, 195-228.

[16]   Chen, N.F. "Financial investment opportunities and the macroeconomy," *Journal of Finance*, (46), 1991, 529-554.

[17]   Chen, N.F. , R. Roll and S. Ross. "Economic forces and the stock market," *Journal of Business*, (59), 1986, 383-403.

[18]   Christopher, Darbyshire. "Survival of the fittest," *Euromoney*, Oct 1991, 43- 48.

[19]   Chung, Kye Sung. "Cracking open Korea's stock exchange," *International Financial Law Review*, Oct 1991, 27-30.

[20]   Claessens Stijn and Gooptu S. "Portfolio Investment in Developing Countries," *World Bank Discussion Papers*, 228, 1993.

[21]   Cochrane, J.H. "How big is the random walk in GNP?," *Journal of Political Economy*, (96), 1988, 893-920.

[22]   Cornelius, Peter K. "Capital controls and market segmentation of emerging stock markets," *Seoul Journal of Economics*, (5), 1992, 289-299.

[23]   Cox, J.C., J.E. Ingersoll and S.A. Ross. "An intetemporal general equilibrium model of asset prices," *Econometrica*, (53), 1985, 363-384.

[24]   Daniel, Kent and Walter Torous. "Common stock returns and business cycle," *Working Paper, University of Chicago*, 1993.

[25]   Dougall, Herbert E. and Jack E. Gaumnitz. "Economic capital and capital formation," *Capital Markets and Institutions*, 5th edition, Englewood Cliffs, NJ: Prentice-Hall, 1986, 1-31.

[26]   Dickey, D.A. and W.A. Fuller. "Likelihood ratio statistics for autoregressive time series with a unit root," *Econometrica*, (49), 1981, 1057-1072.

[27] Errunza Vihang R. and Etienne Losq. "The behavior of stock prices in LDC markets," *Journal of Banking and Finance*, (9), 1985, 561-575.

[28] Fama, E.F. "Efficient capital markets: A review of theory and empirical work," *Journal of Finance*, (25), 1970, 383-417.

[29] Fama, E.F. "Short-term interest rates as predictors of inflation," *The American Economic Review*, (65), 1975, 269-282.

[30] Fama, E.F. "Stock returns, real activity, inflation and money," *American Economic Review*, 1981, 545-565.

[31] Fama, E.F. "The permanent and temporary components in stocks prices," *Journal of Political Economy*, (96), 1988, 247-273.

[32] Fama, E.F. "Stock returns, expected returns and real activity," *Journal of Finance*, (45), 1990, 1089-1108.

[33] Fama, E.F. "Efficient capital markets: II," *Journal of Finance*, (46), 1991, 1575-1617.

[34] Fama, E.F. and K.R. French. "Dividend yields and expected stock returns," *Journal of Financial Economics*, (22), 1988, 3-25.

[35] Fama, E.F. and K.R. French. "Business conditions and expected returns on stocks and bonds," *Journal of Financial Economics*, (25), 1989, 23-49.

[36] Fama E.F. and J.D. MacBeth "Risk, return and equilibrium: Empirical tests," *Journal of Political Economy*, (81), 1973, 607-635.

[37] Fama E.F. and G.W. Schwert "Asset returns and inflation," *Journal of Financial Economics*, (5), 1977, 115-146.

[38] Ferson W.E. and C.R. Harvey. "The variation of economic risk premiums," *Journal of Political Economy*, (99), 1991, 385-415.

[39] Flavin, Marjorie. "Excess volatility in the financial markets: A reassessment of the empirical evidence," *Journal of Political economy*, (91), 1983, 929-956.

[40] Frankel, Jeffrey A. "Foreign exchange policy, monetary policy and capital market liberlization in Korea," *University of California Berkeley, Working Paper No. C93-008*, Jan 1993.

[41] French, K.R. and R. Roll. "Stock return variances: The arrival of information and the reaction of traders," *Journal of Financial Economics*, (17), 1986, 5-27.

[42] French, K.R., G.W. Schwert and R.F. Stambaugh. "Expected stock returns and volatility," *Journal of Financial Economics*, (19), 1987, 3-29.

[43] Friend, Irwin and Marshall Blume. "The demand for risky assets," *American Economic Review*, (65), 1975, 900-922.

[44]   Geweke, John. "Measurement of linear dependence and feedback between multiple time series," *Journal of the American Statistical Association*, (77), 1982, 304-324.

[45]   Grossman, Stanford J. and Robert J. Shiller. "The determinants of the variability of stock prices," *American Economic Review*, (71). 1981, 222-227.

[46]   Grossman, S.J. and R.J. Shiller. "Consumption correlatedness and risk measurement in economies with non traded assets and heterogenous information," *Journal of Financial Economics*, (10), 1982, 195-210.

[47]   Hak, Pyo. "Export led growth, domestic distortions and trade liberlization: the Korean experience during the 1980s," *Journal of Asian Economics*, 1990, 225-247.

[48]   Hall, Robert E. "Stochastic implications of the life cycle-permanent income hypothesis: Theory and evidence," *Journal of Political Economy* (86), 1978, 971-987.

[49]   Hansen, Lars P. and Kenneth J. Singleton. "Generalized instrumental variables estimation of nonlinear rational expectations models," *Econometrica*, (50), 1982, 1269-1286.

[50]   Hansen L.P. and K.J. Singleton. "Stochastic consumption, risk aversion and the temporal behavior of asset returns," *Journal of Political Economy*, (91), 1983, 249-265.

[51]   Siegel, Jeremy (1994). "Stocks for the Long Run(Burr Ridge," *Illinois: Irwin Professional Publishing.*

[52]   Johnston, J. *Econometrics methods*, McGraw Hill, 3rd edition, 1984.

[53]   Jun, K. "The Korean securities market," *Unpublished Manuscript*, World Bank, Aug 1992.

[54]   Keim, D.B. and R.F. Stambaugh. "Predicting returns in the stock and bond markets," *Journal of Financial Economics*, (17), 1986, 357-390.

[55]   Kendall M.G. "The analysis of economic time series, Part I; Prices," *Journal of the Royal Statistical Society*, (96), 1953, 11-25.

[56]   Kindleberger, Charles P. *Maniacs, Panics and Crashes: A History of Financial Crises* 1989, New York: Basic Books.

[57]   Kleidon, Allan W. "Stock prices as rational forecasters of future cash flows," Ph.D. dissertation, University of Chicago.

[58]   Kmenta, Jan. *Elements of econometrics*, New York: Macmillan, 2nd edition, 1986.

[59]   Kon, S.J. and F.C. Jen. "The investment performance of mutual funds: An empirical investigation of timing, selectivity and market efficiency," *Journal of Business*, (52), 1979, 263-289.

[60]   Lee, Byung-Jong. "Capital market: Toward full-fledged liberlization," *Business Korea*, Jan 1989, 41- 53.

[61]   Lee, Keum-Hyun. "Stock market booster: Limping towards liberlization," *Business Korea*, Jan 1990a, 60-62.

[62]   Lee, Keum-Hyun. "Korea's securities market: Chasing financial rivals," *Business Korea*, Apr 1990b, 42-46.

[63]   Lee, Won-Young. "Direct foreign investment in Korea: Pattern, impacts and government policy," *Korean Development Institute, Working Paper No. 8706*, June 1987.

[64]   LeRoy, Stephen F. and William R. Parke. "Stock price volatility: Tests based on the geometric random walk," *American Economic Review*, (82), 1992, 981-992.

[65]   Lo, A.W. and A.C. McKinlay. "Stock market prices do not follow random walks: Evidence from a simple specification test," *Review of Financial Studies*, (1), 1988, 41-66.

[66]   Marathe, Achla and Hany Shawky. "Predictability of Stock Returns and Real Output," *Quarterly Review of Economics and Finance*, vol 34, No. 4, winter 1994, 317-331.

[67]   Marathe, Achla and Edward Renshaw. "Stock Market Bubbles: Some Historical Perspective," *The Journal of Investing*, vol 4, No. 4, winter 1995, 63-73. Also, appeared in the *Neural Networks in Capital Markets* conference, California Institute of Technology, Pasadena, Nov 94.

[68]   Markowitz, Harry M. "Portfolio selection," *Journal of Finance*, (7), 1952, 77-91.

[69]   McCallum, Bennett. *Monetary economics: Theory and policy*, New York: Macmillan, 1989.

[70]   Maddala, G.S. "Introduction to econometrics," second edition, 1992, chapter 13.

[71]   Marsh, Terry A. and Robert C. Merton. "Dividend variability and variance bounds tests for the rationality of stock market prices," *American Economic Review*, (76), 1986, 483-498.

[72]   Merton, Robert C. "On estimating the expected return on the market: An exploratory investigation," *Journal of Financial Economics*, (8), 1980, 323-361.

[73]   Modigliani, F. and R. Brumberg. "Utility analysis and the consumption function" in K. Kurihara, ed: Post Keynesian Economics, 1955.

[74]   Mullin, John. "Emerging equity markets in the global economy," *Federal Reserve Bank of New York Quarterly Review*, Summer 1993, 54-83.

[75]   Nelson, C.R. "Inflation and rates of return on common stocks," *Journal of Finance*, (31), 1976, 471-483.

[76]   Nelson, C.R. and C.I. Plosser. "Trends and random walks in macroeconomic time series," *Journal of Monetary Economics*, (10), 1982, 139-162.

[77]   Officer, Robert R. "The variability of the market factor of New York Stock Exchange," *Journal of Business*, (46), 1973, 434-453.

[78]   Park, Keith K.H. and W.V. Agtmael. "The world's emerging stock markets," *Probus Publishing Company, Chicago, Illinois*, 1993, Chapter 1, 5 and 26.

[79]   Pettit, R.R. "Dividend announcements, security performance and capital market efficiency," *Journal of Finance*, (27), 1972, 993-1007.

[80]   Pindyck, Robert S. "Risk, inflation and the stock market," *American Economic Review*, (74), 1984, 335-351.

[81]   Poterba, James M. and Lawrence H. Summers. "The persistence of volatility and stock market fluctuations," *American Economic Review*, (76), 1986, 1142-1151.

[82]   Poterba, James M. and Lawrence H. Summers. "Mean reversion in stock returns: Evidence and implications," *NBER*, 1987, March.

[83]   Renshaw, Edward (1990). "Some Evidence in Support of Stock Market Bubbles," *Financial Analysts Journal*, March/April, 71-73.

[84]   Renshaw, Edward (1991). "A Formula Plan for a More Volatile Stock Market," *Financial Analysts Journal*, January/February, 85-87.

[85]   Renshaw, Edward, Editor, (1992). "The Practical Forecasters' Almanac," *Burr Ridge, Illinois: Irwin Professional Publishing*.

[86]   Renshaw, Edward (1995a). "There is No Big Picture, Or, That Is the Big Picture," *The Journal of Investing*, Summer, 56-61.

[87]   Renshaw, Edward (1995b). "Is the Stock Market More Stable than it Used to Be?" *Financial Analysts Journal*, Nov./Dec., 81-88.

[88]   Roll, Richard. "Industrial structure and the comparative behavior of international stock market indexes," *Journal of Finance*, (47), 1992, 3-42.

[89]   Romer, David and Matthew D. Shapiro. "An unbiased reexamination of stock market volatility," *Journal of Finance*, (40), 1985, 677-689.

[90]   Ross, Stephen A. "Return, risk and arbitrage," in Irwin Friend and James L. Bicksler, *Risk and return in finance*, Cambridge, MA: Ballinger, 189-218.

[91]   Ryser, Jeffrey. "Turning up their noses at foreign funds," *Global Finance*, Jan 1992, 44-46.

[92]   Santis, Giorgio De. "Asset pricing the portfolio diversification: Evidence from emerging financial markets," *Univ. of Southern California, Unpublished manuscript*, 1993.

[93]   Sargent, Sarah. "Korea waits for the goldrush," *Asia Money and Finace*, Dec 1991-Jan 1992, 19-22.

[94]   Sargent T.J. and N. Wallace "Rational expectations, the optimal monetary instrument and the optimal money supply rule," *Journal of Political Economy*, (83), 1975, 241-254.

[95]   Schwert, William G. "Why does stock market volatility change over time?," *Journal of Finance*, (44), 1989, 1115-1154.

[96]   Schwert, G.W. "Stock returns and real activity: A century of evidence," *Journal of Finance*, (45), 1990, 1237-1258.

[97]   Seyhun, H.N. "Insiders' profits, costs of trading and market efficiency," *Journal of Financial Economics*, (16), 1986, 189-212.

[98]   Sharpe, William F. "Capital asset prices: A theory of market equilibrium under conditions of risk," *Journal of Finance*, (19), 1964, 425-442.

[99]   Shawky, Hany A. "An update on mutual funds: Better grades," *Journal of Portfolio Management*, 1982, 29-34.

[100] Shawky, Hany A. and Achla Marathe. "Expected Stock Returns and Volatility in a Two Regime Market," *Journal of Economics and Business*, vol 47, No. 5, Dec 1995, 409-422.

[101] Shiller, Robert J. "The volatility of long term interest rates and expectations models of the term structure," *Journal of Political Economy*, (87), 1979, 1190-1219.

[102] Shiller, Robert J. "Do stock prices move too much to be justified by subsequent changes in dividends?," *American Economic Review*, (71), 1981a, 421-436.

[103] Shiller, Robert J. "The use of volatility measures in assessing market efficiency," *Journal of Finance*, (36), 1981b, 290-304.

[104] Sidney, Alexander. "Price movements in speculative markets: Trends and random walks," em Industrial Management Review, (2), 1961, 7-26.

[105] Sims, C.A. "Money, Income and Causality," *The American Economic Review*, (62), 1972, 540-552.

[106] Sims, C.A. "Comparisons of interwar and postwar business cycles: Monetarism reconsidered," *American Economic Review*, (70), 1980, 250-257.

[107] Sohn, Jie-ae. "Financial market opening: A hot potato," *Business Korea*, Oct 1991, 36-43.

[108] Tobin, James. "Liquidity preference as behavior towards risk," *The Review of Economic Studies*, (25), 1958, 65-86.

[109] Tobin, James et al. "Volatility in U.S. and Japanese Stock Markets: A Symposium," *Journal of Applied Corporate Finance* (5), 1992, 5-35.

[110] West, Kenneth D. "Dividends innovations and stock price volatility," *Econometrica*, (56), 1988, 37-61.

Index